Coping with Children in Stress

Edited by Ved Varma

arena

Published by
Arena
Ashgate Publishing Limited
Gower House
Croft Road
Aldershot
Hants GU11 3HR
England

Ashgate Publishing Company
Old Post Road
Brookfield
Vermont 05036
USA

British Library Cataloguing in Publication Data

Coping with Children in Stress
  I. Varma, Ved P.
  155.418

Library of Congress Catalog Card Number: 95-83041

ISBN 1 85742 253 8 (paperback)
ISBN 1 85742 252 X (hardback)

Typeset in Palatino by Poole Typesetting (Wessex) Ltd, Bournemouth and printed in Great Britain by Hartnolls Ltd, Bodmin

SSH
(REF)

Contents

v

Figures

Contributors

Maurice Chazan is Emeritus Professor of Education at the University of Wales, Swansea. He has co-directed several research projects and has written extensively on educational disadvantage and emotional and behavioural difficulties. He is a Fellow of the British Psychological Society.

Kedar Nath Dwivedi is Consultant in Child, Adolescent and Family Psychiatry at the Child and Family Consultation Service and the Ken Stewart Family Centre, Northampton. He is also Clinical Teacher in the Faculty of Medicine, University of Leicester.

Joan Freeman is Professor at the University of Middlesex and also Honorary Lecturer at the Institute of Education, University of London. She is a Fellow of the British Psychological Society, and is Founder President of the European Council for High Ability (ECHA), an association which promotes the development of talent during the life span.

Rachel Godfrey is Clinical Psychologist at the Royal National Throat, Nose and Ear Hospital, London. She works with hearing-impaired children and those with speech and language problems as well as adults with tinnitus, vertigo and disorders of hearing.

Anthony Manning works for Redbridge Education Department as Principal Psychiatric Social Worker at the Child and Family Consultation Centre in Ilford. For nearly twenty years he has specialised in clinical work with children and their families in multi-disciplinary team settings.

Christa Schreiber-Kounine is Clinical Psychologist at the United Bristol Healthcare Trust, with special responsibilities for training and continuous professional development. She has previously worked for Camden and Islington Health Authority as a child psychologist, spending five years at the Nuffield Hearing and Speech Centre.

Frank Steel is Headteacher of Rose Hill, Worcester, a special school for children with physical disabilities. Having lectured and written on aspects of special education and contributed material for the distance learning course in learning difficulties which is organised by Birmingham University, he is now a member of the Executive Committee of Hereford and Worcester Lifestyles' Project, and currently chairperson of the Heads of Special Schools and Services Association within Hereford and Worcester.

Juliet Stone was a primary school teacher before working with visually-impaired children in mainstream education. She was a senior advisory teacher for children with special needs in Gloucestershire, having responsibility for all the visually-impaired children and young people in the county. She joined Birmingham University as a trainer of teachers working with visually-impaired children on full-time and distance education courses. She is a trained mobility teacher and has run numerous training courses for teachers across Europe.

Christina Tilstone has taught children with severe learning difficulties for more than thirty years, in a range of special and mainstream schools. She is now Lecturer in Special Education at the University of Birmingham and is currently responsible for the co-ordination of the Learning Difficulties Distance Education Course. She is Editor of the *British Journal of Special Education*.

Ved Varma was formerly an educational psychologist with the Institute of Education, University of London, the Tavistock Clinic, and for the London Boroughs of Richmond and Brent. During the last sixty years he has been no stranger to stressed children and he is a recognised authority on them. He has edited or co-edited more than thirty books in education, psychology, psychiatry, psychotherapy and social work.

John Visser began his teaching career in the primary sector but has experience of secondary and special schools. He is currently at the University of Birmingham where he is responsible for specialist courses in emotional and behavioural difficulties, and learning support. A founder member of the National Association for Special Educational Needs, he has been active nationally in SEN since the 1980s and sits on a number of national committees.

Foreword

David Fontana

In approaching the subject of stress in children, we need to remember two things: firstly that children feel deeply, and secondly that they are often not very good at communicating their feelings to adults. Thus a child may be suffering extreme stress at school or in the home, yet outwardly appear to be coping well with life. In many cases, children are thus expected to continue to function in situations and under pressures which would be tolerated by few adults. All too frequently, it is only in later years, when the wounds of childhood are still causing pain, that the individual looks back and gives voice to the extent of his or her own misery during the most formative period of life.

Things are often made worse for children by the fact that, when they do attempt to communicate their feelings, these are taken less than seriously by parents and teachers. The child is told to stop making a fuss over nothing, to be a man (if male), to think more of others (if female), to stop pestering, to work harder, to obey the teacher, to be a credit to parents, to grow up, and so on. Rarely is the child listened to in the sympathetic way in which we listen to adults in distress, or given credit for having real feelings and for – just possibly – knowing what is wrong with his or her own life, and what needs to be done to put things to rights.

The tragic consequences of this neglect of childhood suffering are seen all around us, not only in potentially high-profile cases involving physical and sexual abuse, but in the largely ignored psychological misery that is the backdrop to many young lives, and which blights present experience and stands in the way of future happiness. One does not need to be a Freudian to recognise the extent to which we carry our childhood with us throughout life, and pay dearly for the mistakes made by caregivers in the early years. For the most part, such mistakes are not, of course, deliberate. They stem from a misunderstanding of childhood, rather than from any real desire to make children's lives difficult. It is surprising how completely many adults forget – or repress – memories of what it was like to be young, and what it was like to lack the power to communicate one's feelings and to influence the tenor of one's life.

Thus this book could not be more timely. It explores each of the situations in which children are likely to experience most stress, and provides practical guidance on how such stress can be minimised and the children concerned provided with the help and support that they need. It honours childhood by recognising its importance, not only as a preparation for the adult years, but as a period of life valid and precious for its own sake. Its approach is sane, sensitive and sensible, and no one who reads it is left in doubt of the moral obligation placed upon us, as adults, to reach a closer understanding of children, and of the factors that make their young lives needlessly difficult. I commend the editor and his collaborators for performing a valuable service, not only for the young, but – because the young are our future – for society as a whole.

Richard Lansdown: An appreciation

Philip Graham

This book is dedicated to Richard Lansdown, and as a long-standing colleague and friend, I am delighted to have been asked to write an appreciation of him.

I first met Richard in 1971, when he applied for the post of Head of Psychology in the Department of Psychological Medicine at the Hospital for Sick Children at Great Ormond Street. Richard seemed to me the best person for the job, though there were other strong candidates. But confirming his appointment was not easy. Richard was an educational psychologist, and hundreds of yards of red tape had to be cleared away to allow his appointment to a clinical post. At one point I nearly gave up, but persistence won through and the appointment was made possible. How right I was not to give up!

Over the past 23 years, Richard has established a reputation as the pre-eminent paediatric psychologist in the UK. I use the term 'paediatric psychologist' to describe someone who is in the business of studying, assessing and treating psychological problems in sick children; and, of course, a children's hospital, although not the only place to carry out such work, is particularly suited to it.

Richard's clinical skills have made his a sought-after opinion – the sort of opinion that paediatricians and child psychiatrists seek for their own children, and there is no better criterion than that. He is particularly good at listening to children who are suffering from chronic, sometimes fatal illnesses, and this has meant he has gained valuable insights into the psychology of the sick child. Talking with sick, even dying, children is a harrowing business, but Richard does not falter – honest and forthright himself, he allows children to be honest with him. He does not push children to tell him about their innermost thoughts and feelings, but they know he is available. Because they can express their fears to him, they can receive as much reassurance as is possible. Those who are responsible for their day-to-day care have their task made easier by such knowledge. However, Richard is not just a psychologist for sick children – at various times in his professional life he has specialised in the learning problems of visually-impaired children (the subject of his PhD thesis), specific reading difficulties (a term I am delighted to report he prefers to dyslexia), and the effects of low-level lead poisoning. He is also an adventurous clinician, interested in new methods of assessment and treatment, and has, for example, promoted the use of techniques such as hypnosis on an experimental basis.

The Institute of Child Health, the Medical School of Great Ormond Street Children's Hospital, runs numerous courses for doctors and other professionals concerned with sick children. Over the years, Richard must have organised and/or spoken on dozens of these courses, as well as lecturing to wider audiences throughout the UK and abroad. He is a superb communicator, and his lectures on talking with dying children, on psychological problems of children with facial deformity, and on other topics in paediatric psychology get the sort of feedback from course participants we all dream about.

Nor is he content to transmit received knowledge. He has been successful in encouraging numerous young psychologists in research projects, especially on subjects relating to the psychological care of sick children. Many of these have been published and have added to our understanding of clinically difficult areas.

Gifted as he is in clinical work, teaching and research, it is as an administrator that Richard's abilities have put him ahead, and indeed out of sight of his contemporaries. He is just *so* organised – it's maddening! Non-medical staff working in hospitals are not usually regarded as even modestly competent to take on major administrative responsibilities – that sort of task is usually reserved for doctors who, sometimes despite considerable evidence to the contrary, regard themselves as fitted by nature to be the only people wise enough to organise other people's work and tell them what to do. At Great Ormond Street Children's Hospital, Richard has not only served as Head of the Department of Psychological Medicine, but, as Director of Neurosciences for several years, he has held the budgets not just for psychiatry and psychology, but for neurology and neurosurgery, neurophysiology and physiotherapy. Richard's administrative abilities have also been recognised on the international scene. For example, he was the Secretary General for the immaculately organised 1982 Dublin meeting of the International Association for Child Psychology, Psychiatry and Allied Professions.

In 1994 Richard left the Hospital for Sick Children, Great Ormond Street, to take up a post as Director of Child to Child, a charity whose work involves the development and dissemination of curriculum material to help older children teach younger children the principles of health education. Now over ten years old, the charity has been successful in establishing numerous programmes in the Third World. Its work is immensely worthwhile, and Richard's many talents will be well employed. Moving back to the educational field, Richard can rest assured he has made a massive contribution to clinical psychology and to our understanding of children under stress – the subject of this book.

Conrad Graham:
An appreciation

Phillip Williams and George Crowther

Every educational psychologist who practised during the 1950s, 1960s and 1970s will remember Conrad Graham. His work with children was characterised by insight and empathy; his research contributions were both timely and valuable. Yet he will be best remembered neither as a clinician nor as a theoretician, but as a key figure in the development of a profession which is centrally concerned with the welfare of children in stress. And, moreover, he will be remembered with great affection.

Conrad is a Londoner, born in 1929. He is of that generation for whom the much-maligned 11+ examination opened the door to a grammar school education, and the first member of his family to enjoy any secondary education at all. His parents both died while he was at school, and he was forced to leave during his first year in the sixth form in order to seek work. At 17, he entered the two-year teacher training course at Goldsmiths' College, leaving with a Class One certificate, a fistful of distinctions, and advice from the staff to take his studies further.

When he was a year into his teaching career, he was admitted to Birkbeck College, where, studying in the evenings and at weekends, he read for an honours degree in psychology. It was here that we first made Conrad's acquaintance. The Birkbeck Psychology Department of the early 1950s was rich in able students, several of whom later became eminent educational psychologists: within a year or so of Conrad were such figures as Mike and Maria Roe and Charles Phillips. By 1954, Conrad had been awarded an Upper Second BSc, gained the Certificate of the Royal Statistical Society, and been admitted to the postgraduate training course for educational psychologists at the University of Birmingham.

At that time, educational psychologists served much larger school populations than today: it was not uncommon for a large education authority serving perhaps 100,000 children to employ a single psychologist. For that reason, psychologists tended to see the children who suffered from more serious problems. Conrad found that working with children with severe emotional distress in the Birmingham schools was itself a traumatic experience, and at the end of his training course he returned to teaching for nearly a year before taking up appointment as an educational psychologist at the Ealing Child Guidance Clinic.

With his statistical background, it was fitting that Conrad's duties should include participating in the 11+ procedure. As with many other psychologists at the time, his role involved advising over 'borderline' children, usually through making individual assessments of their potential as grammar school pupils. This was never easy: the parents saw a recommendation for a secondary modern school as a denial of the opportunities that a grammar school education could offer their child; the children saw themselves as failures. The recommendations could cause great grief and pain, particularly in ambitious families. The task involved combining fairness with humanity – a task to which Conrad was well fitted.

While at Ealing, Conrad registered for a PhD, again at Birkbeck. He chose as the topic for his thesis the relationship between ability and attainment, and this occupied much of his time for the next 14 years, until he submitted his thesis and was awarded his doctorate. Today the topic may seem unexciting, but during the 1960s, when the fiery political debate over selection for secondary education was raging, and when concepts of over- and under-achievement were very controversial, this was a highly-charged theme.

By 1959, Conrad moved to Willesden as Senior Educational Psychologist – a post which the Greater London reorganisation in 1965 re-designated Chief Educational Psychologist for the new Borough of Brent. It could be argued that few psychological services had to work in more difficult circumstances. Into an ethnically mixed area, with settled populations of Irish and Jewish backgrounds, there arrived a huge influx of immigrants from the New Commonwealth, largely from the Caribbean and the Indian sub-continent. The schools were under great pressure, for it was impossible to predict the increase in the number of places required from one week to the next. The teachers, whose classrooms were crowded with newly-arrived pupils from different cultures, many with very limited English, faced problems of learning and behaviour for which they were quite unprepared. They turned to the psychologists.

At that time, help for children with serious learning difficulties was mainly offered through special schools and classes, usually available to children who had been designated 'educationally subnormal'. This was the procedure the psychologists followed. It led to a storm of protest from many parents, culminating in the publication of a Brent-based polemic, *How the*

West Indian Child is made Educationally Subnormal in the British School System.[1] Conrad and his colleagues were in the eye of the storm. The furore led to the establishment by the government of the Rampton[2] and Swann[3] Reports on the education of children from ethnic minorities, and to a rethinking of the procedures for offering help to children with learning difficulties.

During this period the profession of educational psychology matured rapidly. The British Psychological Society (BPS) represented educational psychologists' interests on bodies such as the Soulbury Committee, which then determined matters such as salaries, a role which was not appropriate for a learned society. So a few senior educational psychologists, headed by Jack Wright, took the initiative in forming the Association of Educational Psychologists (AEP). Conrad was a leading member of this group, and was the AEP's first secretary, and later its president. It was a critical time in the history of the profession. The fledgling association might well not have survived the pressure from entrenched interests, and its strength and status today are a tribute to the wisdom and enthusiasm of those pioneers. Conrad's own contributions at that time are too lengthy to list in full. Suffice it to say that for a period he held the post of Secretary to the British Psychological Society's English Division of Professional Psychologists (Education), to the division's Research Committee and to the Association of Educational Psychologists – all at the same time! He was probably the best-known and perhaps the most influential educational psychologist in the country.

Conrad tells a story that, when working in Willesden, he received a school referral which turned out to be probably the most bizarre received by any educational psychologist. An intelligent 15-year-old boy named Graham Young was referred because he had a great interest in poisons. Conrad surmised that the boy was administering poisons to others. In due course, arrangements were made to pass information to the local CID. Graham Young appeared at the Old Bailey and was committed to Broadmoor. Years later he was freed, and shortly afterwards killed three workmates with poison and was sent to prison for life.

During his time in Brent as Chief Educational Psychologist, the School Psychological Service evolved substantially. In his 17 years there, he helped some fifty educational psychology trainees from all parts of the country gain experience. Conrad was a hard taskmaster; he made sure that the trainees were able to convey their psychological investigations and insights in written reports. Conrad has followed the careers of many of his trainees, and he remembers them, and they him, with much fondness and affection.

[1]   Coard, B. (1971) London: New Beacon Books.
[2]   DES (1981) *West Indian Children in our Schools*, London: HMSO (Interim Report of the Rampton Committee into the Education of Children from Ethnic Minority Groups).
[3]   DES (1985) *Education for All*, London: HMSO.

In 1976, Conrad was appointed to the Inner London Education Authority (ILEA), as Inspector of Special Education (District Rank) with special responsibility for children with emotional and behavioural difficulties. The job was quite different from that of an educational psychologist. It did not consist of face-to-face clinical work with children, although the expertise gained from such clinical work was of enormous value, not only with children but also with those who had teaching and childcare responsibilities.

The job was onerous. Some of the inner-city boroughs were among the most deprived in the country – it was a stressful and worrying time. On one occasion, the Chief Inspector of the day, seeing Conrad treading wearily up a County Hall staircase, quipped light-heartedly: 'You ought to develop an interest outside County Hall.' In fact, Conrad's well-balanced view of life and his good sense of humour always saw him through.

In 1984 the ILEA set up working parties to look at secondary, primary and special education. Conrad was honoured to be a member of the Special Education Working Party which produced, in 1985, a substantial report that, however, had little chance of implementation. In 1990 the ILEA was abolished.

Conrad retired in August 1988, when a grand farewell involving his family, friends and colleagues was held in one of the banqueting rooms at County Hall. Now of State Pension age, he continues to lead an active life. He is a movie buff and attends the National Film Theatre regularly. He is also a keen Rotarian and a member of his local Probus Club. An avid collector, he writes the occasional article for stamp, postcard and cigarette card collectors' magazines, and is a specialist in philatelic literature. He has a long-standing interest in history and politics, and his supply of amusing anecdotes shows no sign of abating.

Conrad's wife, Kay, teaches in North London. His son, Robert, is an ergonomist, and his daughter, Carolyn, after graduating in psychology, is about to join the teaching profession.

Conrad's sociability and wide interests have given him an extremely wide circle of friends, nationally and internationally. He is a well-known and highly respected colleague who has brought his considerable influence to bear on children in stress, on their parents who are ultimately responsible for their every-day lives, and on the many professionals who work with them.

Introduction

Ved Varma

All of us have experienced stress at one time or another – in our personal relationships, in our work, in our health, or in a combination of these. It can be argued that stress is likely to be most evident during periods of rapid change, and since childhood is the period during which we develop most rapidly, a strong argument can be made that stress is likely to be prevalent in children. It would seem that as stress is a part of everyday life, the art of living therefore lies in the achieving of equilibrium between a range of stresses. Because the nature and intensity of stresses are constantly changing, an important requirement is the ability to foresee those changes and adjust and adapt to meet them. It follows that learning to live must include experience of stress, experience which must be controlled so that in any situation the stress is enough to challenge, but not so great as to overwhelm. Precise evaluation of stress is usually impossible and one must not assume that a child will have sufficient resilience and tolerance to recover without harm if he should happen to be temporarily overwhelmed. When a child has special needs this is even more important. For some groups of children, stress in childhood is more permanent or more serious than for others, and it is with them that this book concerns itself. (Unfortunately the restrictions of a book of this kind mean that some groups of children have had to be left out – these omissions are regretted.)

At this stage it must be pointed out that 'stress' is a difficult concept to define (several chapters give different definitions and this terminological difficulty is discussed in more depth in Chapter 8). It must also be mentioned that some of these children will be subject to more than one of the range of stressors dealt with in individual chapters. It is also likely that a variety of factors will influence the degree of stress experienced and that some children will be more susceptible than others. With caution, the approaches discussed for coping with one stressor may be applied to others, so that those who deal with, say, visually-impaired children should not necessarily overlook the chapter on hearing impairments. Each perspective complements and enriches the others.

This book provides a broad overview of what is a complex subject. The authors have been included because of their mastery of their individual fields. Most children are brought to us today not because they are 'sick' or 'ill' in the conventional medical sense, but because their problems are ill-defined. They present what Dr Thomas Szasz has quite properly called 'problems of living'. What they all seek is acceptance, insight and knowledge towards better ways of managing their lives. I hope that this volume will play some part in reaching that goal.

1   Learning difficulties

Christina Tilstone and John Visser

Introduction

Most of us, at one time or another, have had problems in learning: mastering a new skill, understanding a new piece of information or acquiring new knowledge in a specific context. Increased awareness of a wide range of learning difficulties led to the Warnock Report (DES, 1978) and resulted in a greater understanding of the effects on the education and progress of children in schools. The Warnock Committee reported that, in its view, 1 in 6 children at any time, and 1 in 5 at some time during their school careers, will require some form of special educational help or support.

This chapter focuses on those children who, as a result of their difficulties, require additional support *most* – and in some cases *all* – of the time. Their difficulties stem from a variety of causes, and they form the 2 per cent of pupils who require highly specialised help.

Despite considerable debate, there is still no general agreement on a precise definition of 'learning difficulty' (Dockrell and McShane, 1993), and the one used by the Warnock Committee has been criticised by authors such as Norwich (1990) as being imprecise:

> We recommend that the term children with learning difficulties should be used to describe both those children who are currently categorised as educationally subnormal and those with educational difficulties who are often at present the concern of the remedial services. (DES, 1978, p.43)

This definition and the legal one given in the subsequent Education Act 1981, and maintained in the Education Act 1993, were also criticised by the Audit Commission (1993). The lack of precision is perhaps understandable when a *difficulty* is only meaningful if it is seen: 'in terms of the interaction of

1

individual pupils' characteristics and needs with the expectations, content and teaching methods of the school' (Gulliford, 1992). Difficulties should not be seen as 'within the child' alone, but as embedded within the policies, curriculum organisation and practices which the school has to offer. As Norwich (1993) emphasises: 'school or teacher difficulties can become learner difficulties' (p.21), and curriculum tasks, activities and classroom learning conditions are often sources of failure and stress.

The fact that some children have learning difficulties makes them more vulnerable to the stresses and strains of every-day life. Like all of us, they differ in their reactions to potentially stressful events, and may cope better on some occasions than on others. Chaplain and Freeman (1994), for example, point out that individuals react in different ways to similar situations, and that they differ considerably both in the levels of stress that they suffer and in their capacity to cope. However, the complex nature of learning difficulties, and the ways in which professionals (including teachers) restrict their pupils' personal powers, underestimate their abilities and undervalue their views, can result in depression, anxiety, strain and stress, none of which are normally experienced by other children in similar contexts.

What is stress?

The terms 'depression', 'anxiety', 'strain' and 'stress' are often used synonymously by teachers, although they have very different parameters. The definitions, as in the case of 'learning difficulties', are often lacking in clarity, and in order to understand the nature of the problems children face and to help them to find solutions, it is important to consider each one separately.

Anxiety is defined in the *Collins English Dictionary* as: 'a state of uneasiness or tension caused by apprehension of possible misfortune or danger'. Contrast this with *depression*: 'a mental disorder characterised by extreme gloom or dejection'. Note that both terms are expressed negatively.

Stress, on the other hand, has a positive dimension – a little can be challenging and invigorating; too much can have negative effects when the pressures become too great for an individual's coping strategies. Dunham (1984) defines it as: 'a process of behavioural, emotional, mental and physical reactions caused by increasing or new pressures which are significantly greater than coping resources' (p.3). As Chaplain and Freeman (1994) point out, stress and coping are two sides of the same coin. If we are coping, we are not stressed, but overstress can result when its demands exceed the individual's limits of adaptability and resourcefulness. Exceeding such limits can result in *burn-out*, when all mental, emotional and physical energies are consumed and exhaustion occurs, and recovery can be a long and complicated process. More serious is the condition termed *strain*, during which the normal limits of endurance are constantly stretched, which can often result in permanent ill health.

As with adults, stress is the child's response to a particular environment or set of circumstances. Limited opportunities and low levels of achievement may be due to restrictive environments, and can result in failure rather than success (Ainscow, 1991). Failure is one of the main causes of stress, and constant failure may lead to a poor self-image and low self-evaluation. The downward spiral moves from stress to failure, from failure to low self-esteem, and from low self-esteem to higher levels of stress.

The symptoms of stress are different for each child, but can be classified as physiological, behavioural or psychological. *Physiological symptoms* can result in muscle tension; aching limbs; headaches; skin disorders and allergies; bowel and bladder disorders, and excessive sweating. *Behavioural disorders* manifest themselves in a proneness to accidents; aggressiveness; absenteeism; restlessness, and withdrawal. *Psychological symptoms* can include obsessions; fear and panic; reduced self-esteem, and a lack of enthusiasm.

Factors causing stress

Physical conditions

As many of the *symptoms* of stress are already present in children with learning difficulties and stem directly from the disabilities themselves, the identification of stress as a factor is not easy. Sensory difficulties or motor dysfunction (which some children experience as part of their physical limitations) or health problems can result in physiological symptoms. The challenging behaviours displayed by some pupils (aggression towards themselves or others or complete withdrawal) may be due to poor levels of language development, the inability to comprehend rules and conventions, or, in a few extreme cases, neurological disturbances which may not be under voluntary control. Only in rare syndromes, however, is there firm evidence to indicate that organic behaviour and challenging behaviour are unequivocally linked (Fraser and Rao, 1991). Some can produce stress-like symptoms, and it is recognised, for example, that children with Prader-Willi syndrome may eat excessively, and those with frontal-lobe epilepsy may have sudden, uncontrollable rages owing to extreme degrees of brain dysfunction.

Physical disabilities (see Chapter 4) are potential causes of stress. The effects of some low-incidence physical conditions have only recently become identified – or, perhaps more accurately, discussed – and consequently, it is essential to consider them in addition to those which are well-documented.

HIV and learning difficulties

The stress experienced by children with HIV and AIDS (both low-incidence physical conditions) has received little coverage. Some of these children have learning difficulties, and as HIV spreads to the heterosexual population, it is no longer possible to focus only on those groups (homosexuals, haemophiliacs and drug abusers) identified as 'at risk' in the 1970s and 1980s; now the population as a whole must be considered at risk. Miles (1993) and Russell (1992) emphasise that, as HIV/AIDS become everyone's concern, schools must be included in the support network. In discussing the scale of the problem, Newell and Peckham (1993) state that, of the 65,000 sufferers from AIDS reported in the UK at the end of 1991, 3,000 were children under 13 years of age. Sexual abuse can be a factor in the spread of the disease, and as Williams (1992) reported, 1 in 4 people with learning difficulties had been sexually abused – a statistic which has serious implications, as much of the abuse is likely to occur in childhood.

Children with AIDS may have learning difficulties for the reasons already identified, but some who are HIV-positive at birth may, as part of the condition, develop neurological problems and learning difficulties. Research (Batty, 1993) indicates that the needs of children with HIV/AIDS are similar to those facing loss and separation. At a basic level, they can be identified as:

- a trusted person to talk to;
- information on the condition, appropriate to the child's age and level of understanding;
- permission to be angry or sad.

Any child suffering from HIV/AIDS may be subject to stress for a variety of reasons, the most common of which are prejudice and discrimination. Children with learning difficulties often suffer from the negative attitudes both of society and of involved professionals, but when HIV is diagnosed, the pressures increase. Cases have been recorded in the UK of children being withdrawn from school when it became known that they were HIV-positive (Viinikka, 1993), and it should be borne in mind that there are strict rules on confidentiality, and that teachers who divulge such information are committing a disciplinary offence. It will be interesting to see whether a greater understanding of children's rights and of legislation such as the Children Act 1989 will mean that children suffering from HIV/AIDS (and their parents) bring actions to enforce their right to attend a neighbourhood school (as is not uncommon in the USA).

Although much can be achieved by challenging the attitudes of the general public, only an adequately funded programme of health education for people with learning difficulties can ensure that the effects of stress, ignorance and fear are alleviated. Mencap is one of the organisations that has attempted to reinforce learning about the transmission of HIV by using board or computer games, which use visual images of real-life situations to encourage young people to make their own decisions regarding what is *safe* and what can be made *safer*.

In the main, teachers are badly served in their efforts to help these children. Not all local education authorities have issued guidelines to schools on how to deal with pupils who are HIV-positive, and government awareness programmes have not been popular as they have been considered mechanistic. In the more enlightened local authorities, policies include the dissemination of basic information on good hygiene practice, with clear instructions to teachers on dealing with blood spillage and cuts and grazes. Training for lunchtime supervisors and support staff is available, and governors receive advice and help on drawing up school policies in line with the local authority guidelines. The need for strict rules of confidentiality is emphasised, and it is the parents' responsibility to choose which members of staff should be told about the condition. By allowing staff to be given information, families can be open about such routine situations as hospital appointments, and consequently their own stress (and that of their children) can be alleviated. The number of support groups and organisations is growing, and some are producing excellent resources. Swinden (1993) singles out a set of lesson cards for primary school children, produced by TACADE, giving the facts about HIV/AIDS, addressing the misconceptions and prejudices, and offering help and support. This set could well be used with older pupils with learning difficulties.

Other low-incidence conditions

Pain and discomfort are themselves disabling in some low-incidence conditions (haemophilia, sickle-cell anaemia, thalassaemia, cancer and acute diabetes) and can result in high levels of stress. Although their incidence is not abnormally high in children with learning difficulties, some – like sickle-cell anaemia and thalassaemia – may necessitate special school placements (Dyson, 1986). Children suffering from AIDS, or who are HIV-positive, may also suffer from pain. Much has been written on the effects of pain on adults, but there has been relatively little research on how children cope. Although many children's health problems involve a variety of painful experiences, which can vary enormously and are subjective, Hall's research (1992) emphasises that adults often underestimate the intensity of children's pain. Fear, ignorance, incomplete diagnosis and inadequate management are factors which will inevitably contribute to a child's stress. Add to these a situation where an adult is inadvertently insensitive to a child's needs or feelings, and the stress factor can be extremely high. The Children Act 1989 emphasises the importance of listening to and learning from children, and the Code of Practice (DFE, 1994) places emphasis on consulting children when identifying, assessing and providing for their special educational needs. Creating opportunities for a child to communicate his or her feelings and wishes is the first step towards understanding and, consequently, alleviating stress. Effective communication depends on contact and interaction, during which some children will rely almost exclusively on non-verbal signals – facial expressions, looks, touch, gestures, and posture – and much can be learned from the basic pain measurement tools used by paediatric nurses. Photographs of children in varying degrees of distress have been used in schools to encourage children with limited verbal skills to indicate their level of discomfort. Such vital information should be passed to medical personnel and has, in some schools, formed part of a comprehensive assessment for an ongoing pain management programme. As it is believed that relaxation can reduce pain by decreasing the effects of stress, some teachers use the basic techniques of encouraging young children to cuddle a favourite toy, singing or talking to them in a soothing voice, or playing them soft music. Massage and aromatherapy have also been successfully used to relax children with learning difficulties (see Sanderson et al., 1991, for an excellent introduction).

Family tensions

The effects on families of children with learning difficulties are determined by individual family dynamics and the nature and severity of the disability. A child with learning difficulties can present practical as well as emotional problems, including the financial burdens of higher than average laundry costs, specialised clothing, and equipment designed specifically for the child with profound and multiple learning difficulties. In addition, one parent may need to stay at home in order to look after the child, limiting the opportunities for both partners to become wage-earners. Inordinate demands on time and energy can become major factors in the isolation of parents and their lack of contact with the community at large. Nevertheless, the emotional problems common in most families of children with learning disabilities are often caused by the pressures of adjustment to the disability. The discrepancy between the *expected* and the *real* can produce intense emotional reactions which are not only stressful to the parents and siblings, but can also produce stress in the child.

Wade and Moore (1993), in one of the few books which focus on the views of children with special educational needs, provide clear proof that feelings of rejection and exclusion begin at home. When children between 7 and 16 years of age with special needs were asked the question, 'I wish my parents would … ?', the range of replies indicated a desire for more care and understanding: ' ... be kind to me'; ' ... give me more love'; ' ... stand by me', and ' ... help me when I'm sick' (p.70). Other responses revealed a desire for improved relationships: ' ... not shout at me'; ' ... stop treating me like a baby'; ' ... be happy with my work' (p.69). The authors state that there may be many reasons why these children feel that their parents do not care (some of which may be concerned with the normal process of growing up), but they emphasise the importance of providing a loving and secure school environment if children feel that they are 'short-changed' at home.

Hornby (1994) discusses models of adaptation to disability in depth, identifying such reactions as shock, denial, anger, sadness and detachment. It has also been reported that parents and other family members suffer greater stress than the parents of non-disabled children, and as a consequence, the whole family can be seen as 'disabled' (Booth, 1978; Beckman, 1984). Hornby (1994) and McConachie (1994) suggest that the focus of research into the effects of a child's disability on his or her family has changed over the last twenty years. Research into childhood disability in the 1990s (McConachie, 1994) identifies the chronic stressors for parents of all children as broken nights, behaviour problems in childhood, and ill health. However, these may have a more intense effect on the families of children with learning difficulties, as broken nights may continue for a longer period, behaviour problems may last into middle childhood or beyond, and the child may be more susceptible to illness. Normal life-events have also been identified as short-term stressors: children entering school, the death of a relative, or illness in the family (McConachie, 1991). These events can become more complex when, for example, a decision has to be reached on whether the child should enter either a mainstream or a special school. Thus, stresses within the family will inevitably add to (or in some cases, bring about) stress in the child with learning difficulties. When a child is regarded as the cause of the problems within a family, his or her reactions to stressful situations are likely to be pronounced. However, if his or her difficulties are regarded as normal and temporary and can be overcome, it is unlikely that family tensions will cause stress.

Society's attitudes

In our competitive society, learning difficulties are still seen as a stigma and a cause of embarrassment. Attitudes to learning difficulties are formed by our own experiences and by what we have absorbed from others. Sandow (1994) summarises the models or sets of beliefs which have informed thinking as:

- *the magical model*, when fears and superstitions lead to the persecution and ridicule of those who are disabled or limited in any way;
- *the moral model*, which suggests that 'mankind is perfectible, and it is his responsibility to become as perfect as possible' (p.2);

- *the medical model,* in which people with learning difficulties ('handicaps') are seen as being in need of care and protection and are often segregated from society; segregated provision (in an institution or asylum) was, in the past, run by doctors who became the experts in dealing with all aspects of their patients' development (Tilstone, 1991);
- *the intellectual model,* which has resulted in intelligence tests being used to determine performance in all areas of development; children with low mental scores were thought not only to be intellectually inferior, but also socially and emotionally immature;
- *the social competence model,* which requires children to conform to the behaviours recognised as important at a particular time in the development of society;
- *the social conspiracy model,* in which it is suggested that the 'normal' is defined by the 'abnormal'; Sandow uses arguments put forward by sociologists (for example, Tomlinson, 1982) to suggest that children with special needs (particularly the 2 per cent mentioned by Warnock, who are the subject of this chapter) require a 'special needs industry' of special teachers, special testers (educational psychologists) and special supporters (the multidisciplinary team).

It is likely that every individual's belief system is influenced by an amalgamation of some or even all of these models, and that the more technologically advanced the society, the narrower the range of intellectual, physical, sensory and emotional abilities considered normal, and therefore acceptable (Fraser, 1984). Children with learning difficulties who could cope with education and life in an underdeveloped country, for example, are perceived as being in need of special treatment in our apparently more sophisticated society. Generally, society's attitudes dictate that children's abilities and potential are not decided by any objective assessment of their achievements, but by negative feelings, emotions, and opinions stirred up in us and influenced by historical trends. The stereotypical images and labels, which form part of public degradation and from which many children suffer from birth, are recognised sources of stress. Many of us can remember the effects of being called 'thick', 'stupid', 'an idiot' or 'hopeless' at some point in our lives, but to be perpetually referred to in this way is a constant reminder of personal 'inadequacy', and will reinforce feelings of failure and rejection, which are in themselves stressful.

It is difficult to change attitudes, but if we are serious about helping children with learning difficulties to reduce their levels of stress, we cannot sit back and hope for the best! Research on shaping community attitudes (McConkey and McCormack, 1983) provides two important suggestions for work in this area – firstly, any attempt to prepare communities or groups to accept others whom they perceive as 'different' will have positive effects; secondly, positive experiences shape positive attitudes.

Structured attitude change is likely to be most effective if ordinary children are introduced to those with learning difficulties at an early age. Lindoe (1991), using CARA (Community Attitudes to Retarded Adults) materials developed by McConkey et al. (1983) in her work with mainstream secondary pupils, outlines a programme of shared activity between her pupils and those with learning difficulties, based on their common interests (football, pop music or art), and emphasises that casual and informal contacts are rarely productive. Using a simple questionnaire, she assessed what the children understood about learning difficulties, and challenged their perceptions by showing videos and films of children with learning difficulties in a range of situations. The use of films and videos also allowed the pupils to *stare* and ask questions. 'Sanctioned staring' alleviates the feelings of discomfort felt when we first meet someone who is physically different or whose behaviour indicates 'slowness'. She argues that unease, discomfort and uncertainty can be reduced and positive feelings developed by providing opportunities for children to share common interests. The pupils in the study no longer regarded the children with learning difficulties as different and handicapped, and began to see them as people with their own personalities, enthusiasms and interests. McConkey (1991) stresses that a vital key to successful community education is to work on target groups in ways similar to those outlined by Lindoe. In his view, global information programmes may make the general public more enlightened about the causes of the problems, but can highlight the *disability* and 'will not produce volunteers for the summer leisure scheme' (McConkey, 1991, p.167).

School factors

For many children with learning difficulties, school is not the enriching experience that it should be, and too often it becomes a major source of stress. Schools differ in their environment, their organisation, their approaches to teaching, and above all in how they value pupils who have difficulties in learning. As Barton (1993) points out, 'competition' and 'choice' have become slogans, and the extent to which schools are 'welcoming institutions to all pupils irrespective of disability, race, gender or class' is being seriously challenged (p.39). At present, many of the pupils who are the subject of this chapter are educated in special schools, and although it is inappropriate to rehearse the arguments for and against segregation, it should be stressed that special needs provision is at a critical stage in its development. Teachers are beginning to state publicly that, owing to the multiple changes demanded by recent legislation and the consequent conflicting pressures, they regard the more able pupils as their priority and are unable to spare the time or energy for those with moderate or severe learning difficulties. Vlachou and Barton (1994) provide useful insights into teachers' feelings about what they see as the 'value-for-money mentality in educational planning and practice'. The views of this teacher are typical:

> my first priority is for all mainstream children and you know a lot of them have got special needs, they need so much help and you have thirty of those children and then you have to deal with the others as well. You try to devote so much time and energy to the mainstream children, you really cannot afford the plus energy that is needed for the special needs children. ('Mrs N', p.107)

Despite the rhetoric and the abundance of legislation centring on special needs over the last few years, it is revealing to compare this comment with a quotation taken from a book written almost thirty years ago by Clegg and Megson (1968) about stress in children:

> But in many, indeed in most schools, what is done is done with the bright child in mind, and parents, teachers, the press and indeed the whole system conspires to this end; because in its heart of hearts this age believes that the child with a modest ability does not really count. Blessed are they who add most to the gross national product. If we take this view, no amount of material provision will give the slower children the support they need, and the schools of this country will make their own contribution to what may well be one of the most grievous social problems of the twentieth century. (p.59)

It seems that nothing has changed!

Many of the mainstream or special in-school factors which bring about stress in children with learning difficulties are well documented. Examination or assessment pressures, bullying, racial discrimination and the effects of high staff turnover are causes of which teachers and other school staff are fully aware. But other, less frequently publicised, factors produce worry, frustration and stress in children, including:

- vulnerable times of the day;
- challenging behaviour on the part of other pupils;
- unexpected events.

Vulnerable times of the day   Playtimes, the beginning and end of lessons and sessions, and movement from one activity to another are all potential sources of stress. Blatchford and Sharp (1994) list the stresses which can be experienced at mealtimes and suggest a range of strategies to avoid them. 'Shadowing' pupils over an extended period, at the times when movement in the building is at its peak, is an effective way of assessing levels of stress resulting from the 'hidden curriculum'. Hargreaves (1982) identified the 'hidden curriculum' as those events and situations not planned, nor intended, by teachers, but which communicate hidden messages concerning attitudes and values to their pupils. In our experience of pupils with a range of learning difficulties, the most stressful time of the day is the early morning, when stress factors relating to the home affect the child in school. It is not easy for parents to cope with a child who is cognitively (and possibly physically) slow but who needs to practise the skills of independence first thing in the morning. At this time there may be other children to get to school, household tasks to undertake, and for some, the need to get ready for work themselves; others may have to undertake all these tasks alone or unsupported. School is the place where the child may off-load or display the results of such pressures, but what happens if a school adds its own pressures by not being a friendly environment or ready to receive the child?

An additional problem may be experienced by parents who have to work unsociable hours in order to maintain their families and their homes. One primary school head was concerned about the increasing number of children left at school very early in the morning, including some with learning diffi-culties. After observing them wandering around the building or huddled in the corners of a dark, cold playground, she and her staff started a breakfast club. Parents pay a small daily fee and can drop their children off up to an hour before school starts, and the children are encouraged to take part in structured activities in a relaxed atmosphere. Such a positive response to a particular situation helped the children to acquire good feelings about them-selves, and the welcome at a normally unsociable time signalled that they were respected and valued. Not all schools will have the need or resources to respond to such demands in the same way, but the procedures schools adopt and the time taken to welcome pupils each morning are crucially important in raising self-esteem. Teachers need to assess how well the school, as an organisation, promotes feelings of self-worth, and to formulate whole-school policies in order to promote self-esteem. However, Moseley (1994), who has written extensively on programmes aimed at developing self-esteem in pupils with special needs, emphasises that the day-to-day respect shown to them by teachers, in all situations, is as important as the policies themselves.

Some children will suffer stress if they cannot detect the clues which help them to make sense of their environment. An excellent example of how a teacher planned an introduction to the school day for a child who has visual and hearing difficulties is given by Wyman (1986):

- '*Off the Bus*. Rana's name is called before she is touched and then handled slowly, so as to give her time to appreciate her teacher's greeting.'
- '*Carried*. Close contact is essential; this gives a sense of well being at the start of the day.'

- '*Stopping*. At the doorway Rana is given time to feel the change of air flow.'
- '*Trailing*. Rana needs me to put her hand to the wall as we move along, to stop at landmarks (the fish tank, the mirror).'
- '*Listening*. This allows time for Rana to pick out the sounds of her own classroom.'
- '*Consistent positioning*. Doors and furniture should remain in the same position; the door should be closed so that we can push it open together.' (pp.176–7)

The teacher used the same approach each day and capitalised on recurring situations in order to enable Rana to anticipate events: ritual and routine are important tools for combating stress, as they give shape to the day and make it predictable. Chaplain and Freeman (1994), who emphasise that rituals are both participatory and communal, found in their research into stress in children in residential settings that security and belonging are the results of the following aspects of the ritual:

- 'time – which can be biological, sequential, chronological or historical'
- 'action – gesture, posture and movement'
- 'space – who controls it and how it is used'
- 'ritual objects and substances – food, cutlery for instance'
- 'power and leadership – who have control over the rituals, how these are used, and how power is established'
- 'discourse – verbal interactions'. (p.127)

Rituals and routines are soothing for staff as well as for pupils, and there is a danger that they may become unquestioned and unevaluated survival skills. Sebba et al. (1993) warn us that such practices can turn into symbols of staff control over pupils.

Challenging behaviour on the part of other pupils   The challenging behaviours displayed by some pupils are not only the symptoms but also the *causes* of stress in others, and it is important to focus on this often unrecognised aspect. In the past, children who exhibited intolerable behaviour were labelled 'disruptive', a term which places the responsibility for the difficulty on the individual pupil, although, in certain circumstances, the behaviour may be due to external factors. The term 'challenging behaviour' has value in that it suggests that problems arise in the interactions between the child and others, and as a consequence, focuses on the ability of teachers, parents and other children to find acceptable ways of tolerating it (Ashdown, 1994). Unfortunately, the challenging behaviours given the most attention are those considered violent or aggressive, although the extent to which they are challenging depends on the tolerance level of individual pupils. McBrien and Felce (1992) categorise challenging behaviour as follows:

- aggression towards others (hitting, kicking, pulling people over);
- self-injury (head-banging, eye-poking, hand-biting);
- destructiveness (breaking windows, throwing objects, ripping books or clothes);
- anti-social (screaming, running away, stripping);
- stereotyped behaviour and self-stimulation (body-rocking, pacing, repetitive noises).

Pupils with moderate and severe learning difficulties are not unique in presenting behaviours which challenge, and Clements (1987) emphasises that conduct problems (aggression, impulsiveness and extreme frustration) are common in many children in ordinary schools at one time or another, and that tantrums and non-compliance are present in most pre-school children. However, challenging behaviour seems to last longer and be more intense in children with learning difficulties, and research shows that the more severe the difficulty, the more challenging the behaviour (Murphy and Oliver, 1987). Unfortunately, the more frequently the behaviour occurs, the more it affects the stress levels of other people within the school, including other children. As one headteacher of a school for pupils with severe learning difficulties reported:

> the behaviour of one pupil is so intense that it sends shock waves to all other pupils in the school, and totally immobilizes pupils in her own class. They are too frightened to move, and many of them show symptoms of stress after the outbursts.

The whole-school approach to the problem, Circle Time (Moseley, 1994), included not only strategies and plans to deal with the behaviour directly, but provided additional support for other children. Circle Time is the name given to a democratic and creative method of problem-solving, which helps children to build trusting relationships and to tackle current difficulties. Circle Time may be used imaginatively in a range of stressful situations, but in this case, children were gathered together in a circle with the sole aim of expressing anxiety and relieving stress. The circle offers a *safe* place, where each child can feel acknowledged and can be *listened to*. It operates within agreed guidelines, and normally children take it in turns to speak and to bring their concerns to the circle. The learning difficulties of the children in this group were such that many of them were at early stages of language development, and non-verbal means had to be employed to allow them to express their feelings. Through the use of puppets and simple Makaton signs, the teacher re-enacted the challenging behaviour drama. She then showed each child a picture of him or herself with the child who had challenged in a happy situation – for example, on a swing or in the ball pool. Time was allowed for each child to respond or react in any appropriate way. Clear pictures were then introduced, showing first sad and then happy faces. Each child was given a glove puppet, and with the help of the staff, a ritualistic play was performed, focusing on sad and happy events. Again, time was allowed for each child to respond in any way possible. Finally, the child who had challenged was re-introduced into the group and lullabies were sung together. At all times the circle provided an effective and *safe* forum to help children to work through their concerns.

In many schools, Circle Times are held weekly and last on average for half an hour. The circle can be a place where achievements are celebrated and problems solved. Moseley (1994) emphasises that the successes are improvements in relationships at all levels and the promotion of personal and collective responsibility.

Unexpected events   One of the most traumatic events that can occur in a mainstream or a special school is the death of a pupil. One of the authors has vivid memories of being told, forty years ago, that a friend in her class had been killed in an accident. The death of children who are attending mainstream schools is, thankfully, a rare occurrence, but children in special schools are, in the main, the most physically frail, and although medical advances have enabled those with profound and multiple learning difficulties to survive the complications of early life, children do die, and the effect on their peers can be devastating. It has often been assumed that pupils with severe learning difficulties are unable to understand death and are therefore unable to grieve. Research shows that they go through the same stages of grief as others (Crick, 1988; Oswin, 1981). Bereavement in itself is painful, but if children's right to grieve is denied, chronic stress can occur. It is likely that the friendship bonds of children with learning difficulties are stronger than we realise. Children may have been in each other's company for most of their school careers, and some of the young people in one of our classes were friends not only in school, but also in the hostel in which they lived. A death in this situation is as painful as the loss of a close family friend. Teachers and school staff have an obligation to meet the needs of young people when they themselves are going through the grieving process – an unenviable task. The strategies developed for use with able pupils are equally applicable to pupils with learning difficulties, although they may need to be modified. Brown (1994) suggests that they should include:

- 'being as open and as honest as possible, especially where children ask questions';
- 'being able to listen or talk or spend time with each child';

- 'talking about the person who has died; keeping their memory alive';
- 'allowing children to show their grief in whatever way they want, (including permission to laugh) and as often as they want'. (p.3)

We would also like to add:

- sharing emotions and grief.

Brown emphasises the use of 'memory boxes' as one tried and tested way of preventing stress and allowing children with severe learning difficulties to come to terms with their grief. The following tangible reminders have proved particularly comforting:

- recent photographs;
- greetings cards sent to, or received from, the child;
- an item of clothing;
- a video or an audio cassette of the child or of a favourite tune;
- a book made about the child (rather like a record of achievement);
- a tactile item – a cup, blanket or special cushion, for example.

Finally, the grieving process must not be rushed. In an effort to 'get back to normal', it is possible that we may be putting undue pressures on pupils and causing even more stress.

Conclusion

Throughout this chapter we have endeavoured to highlight some of the causes of stress which are not often talked about. When pupils are consulted about what they consider to be their most serious problems, their answers are often surprising. The most effective way of detecting individual problems is through systematic observation. Observing and recording the physical, behavioural and psychological signs of stress is an excellent starting point. Resource material is available for teachers in mainstream schools (for example, Mills, 1992), and much of it can be successfully adapted for work with pupils with learning difficulties.

Even the very best resource packs will not alone enable teachers to cope with stress in children. The most powerful tool lies in the curriculum itself. The statutory responsibility that the Education Reform Act 1988 places on schools to provide a broad and balanced curriculum which promotes the spiritual, moral, cultural, mental and physical development of pupils at the school and of society, and prepares pupils for the opportunities, responsibilities and experiences of adult life (p.1), must be seen as the starting point for promoting the balanced development of children and the means by which they are able to take control of their own lives. We are, of course, looking beyond the subjects of the National Curriculum towards those aspects of the total curriculum which ensure the maturity of the whole child. Sebba et al. (1993) emphasise – as does the NCC (1990a) document, *The Whole Curriculum* – that children's personal and social development must be the main aim of education, and that it can only be achieved through personal and social education. It is to our advantage that there are no attainment targets or programmes of study laid down for personal and social education, although its components can be identified in the dimensions, skills and themes which make up the cross-curricular elements (see NCC, 1990a; 1990b; 1990c; 1990d). The activities and tasks which are necessary for personal and social education offer teachers unique opportunities to observe and to listen to children. The Children Act, too, requires us to listen, and the Code of Practice (DFE, 1994) emphasises that children have a right to be heard throughout their education, and that their wishes should be taken into account. In an effort to address the stress-related needs of children with learning difficulties, teachers and other professionals must learn to *listen* carefully. For once, current legislation is working to our advantage.

Acknowledgement

The authors wish to thank Rob Ashdown for his invaluable advice on the section 'Challenging behaviour on the part of other pupils'.

References

Ainscow, M. (1991) 'Effective Schools for All: An Alternative Approach to Special Needs Education', in Ainscow, M. (ed.) *Effective Schools for All*, London: David Fulton.

Ashdown, R. (1994) 'Challenging Behaviour', in Tilstone, C. (ed.) *Distance Learning Course for Teachers of Children with Learning Difficulties (Moderate and Severe)*, Birmingham: University of Birmingham.

Audit Commission (1993) *Getting in on the Act*, London: HMSO.

Barton, L. (1993) 'Labels, markers and inclusive education', in Visser, J. and Upton, G. (eds) *Special Education in Britain After Warnock*, London: David Fulton.

Batty, D. (ed.) (1993) *HIV Infection and Children in Need*, London: British Agencies for Adoption and Fostering.

Beckman, P.J. (1984) 'A transactional view of stress in families of handicapped children', in Lewis, M. (ed.) *Beyond the Dyad*, New York: Plenum Press.

Blatchford, P. and Sharp, S. (1994) *Breaktime and the School*, London: Routledge.

Booth, T. (1978), 'From normal baby to handicapped child: unravelling the idea of subnormality in families of handicapped children', *Sociology*, No. 12.

Brown, E. (1994) 'Mentally Handicapped Children and Death', *RESPECT*, No. 8, Spring, p.3.

Chaplain, R. and Freeman, A. (1994) *Caring Under Pressure*, London: David Fulton.

Clegg, A. and Megson, B. (1968) *Children in Distress*, Harmondsworth: Penguin.

Clements, J.C. (1987) *Severe Learning Disabilities and Psychological Handicap*, Chichester: John Wiley.

Crick, L. (1988) 'Facing Grief', *Nursing Times*, Vol. 84, No. 28, pp.61–3.

DES (Department of Education and Science) (1978) *Special Educational Needs: Report of the Committee of Inquiry into the Education of Handicapped Children and Young People*, London: HMSO (The Warnock Report).

DFE (Department for Education) (1994) *Identifying and Assessing Special Educational Needs*, London: Department for Education.

Dockrell, J. and McShane, J. (1993) *Children's Learning Difficulties: A Cognitive Approach*, Oxford: Blackwells.

Dunham, J. (1984) *Stress in Teaching*, London: Croom Helm.

Dyson, S. (1986) 'Professionals, mentally handicapped children and confidential files', *Disability, Handicap and Society*, Vol. 1, No. 1, pp.73–87.

Fraser, B. (1984) *Society, Schools and Handicap*, Stratford: National Council for Special Education.

Fraser, W.I. and Rao, J.M. (1991) 'Recent studies of mentally handicapped people's behaviour', *Journal of Child Psychology and Psychiatry*, Vol. 32, No. 1, pp.79–108.

Gulliford, R. (1992) 'Learning difficulties', in Gulliford, R. and Upton, G. (eds) *Special Educational Needs*, London: Routledge.

Hall, N. (1992) 'Psychological and health-related problems', in Gulliford, R. and Upton, G. (eds) *Special Educational Needs*, London: Routledge.

Hargreaves, D. (1982) *The Challenge of the Comprehensive School: Culture, curriculum and community*, London: Routledge and Kegan Paul.

Hornby, G. (1994) *Counselling in Child Disability*, London: Chapman and Hall.

Lindoe, S. (1991) 'Integration: Planned interaction – the first steps', in Tilstone, C. (ed.) *Teaching Pupils with Severe Learning Difficulties*, London: David Fulton.

McBrien, J. and Felce, D. (1992) *Working with People who have Severe Learning Disability and Challenging Behaviour: A Practical Handbook on the Behavioural Approach*, Clevedon: BIMH Publications.

McConachie, H. (1991) 'Families and professionals: Prospects for partnership', in Segal, S. and Varma, V. (eds) *Prospects for People with Learning Difficulties*, London: David Fulton.

McConachie, H. (1994) 'Implications of a model of stress and coping services to families of young disabled children', *Child Care, Health and Development*, No. 20, pp.37–46.

McConkey, R. (1991) 'Changing the public's perception of mental handicap', in Segal, S. and Varma, V. (eds) *Prospects for People with Learning Difficulties*, London: David Fulton.

McConkey, R. and McCormack, B. (1983) *Breaking Barriers: Educating the Public About Disability*, London: Souvenir Press.

McConkey, R., McCormack, B. and Naughton, M. (1983) *CARA Project Information Pack*, Dublin: St Michael's House Research/Health Education Bureau.

Miles, M. (1993) 'Introduction', in Batty, D. (ed.) *HIV Infection and Children in Need*, London: British Agencies for Adoption and Fostering.

Mills, S. (1992) *Helping Pupils to Cope with Stress: A Guide for Teachers*, Lancaster: Framework Press.

Moseley, J. (1994) 'Developing Self-Esteem', *Special Children*, No. 74, April.

Murphy, G. and Oliver, C. (1987) 'Decreasing undesirable behaviours', in Yule, W. and Carr, J. (eds) *Behaviour Modification for People with Mental Handicaps* (2nd edn), London: Croom Helm.

National Curriculum Council (1990a) *Curriculum Guidance 3: The Whole Curriculum*, York: NCC.

National Curriculum Council (1990b) *Curriculum Guidance 5: Health Education*, York: NCC.

National Curriculum Council (1990c) *Curriculum Guidance 6: Careers, Education and Guidance*, York: NCC.

National Curriculum Council (1990d) *Curriculum Guidance 8: Education for Citizenship*, York: NCC.

Newell, M. and Peckham, C. (1993) 'Transmission of HIV Infection', in Batty, D. (ed.) *HIV Infection and Children in Need*, London: British Agencies for Adoption and Fostering.

Norwich, B. (1990) *Reappraising Special Needs in Education*, London: Cassell.

Norwich, B. (1993) 'Towards Effective Schools for All: A Response', in Ainscow, M. (ed.) *Towards Effective Schools for All*, Stafford: National Association for Special Educational Needs.

Oswin, M. (1981) *Bereavement and Mentally Handicapped People: A Discussion Paper*, London: Kings Fund.

Rose, R., Fergusson, A., Coles, C., Byers, R. and Banes, D. (eds) (1994) *Implementing the Whole Curriculum for Pupils with Learning Difficulties*, London: David Fulton.

Russell, P. (1992) 'Affected by HIV and AIDS: Cameos of young people', in Booth, T., Swann, W., Masterton, M. and Potts, P. (eds) *Curricula for Diversity in Education*, London: Routledge.

Sanderson, H., Harrison, J. and Price, S. (1991) *Aromatherapy and Massage for People with Learning Difficulties*, Birmingham: Hands on Publishing/Shirley Price Publishing.

Sandow, S. (ed.) (1994) *Whose Special Need?*, London: Paul Chapman.

Sebba, J., Byers, R. and Rose, R. (1993) *Redefining the Whole Curriculum for Pupils with Learning Difficulties*, London: David Fulton.

Swinden, L. (1993) 'Tales of the unprotected', *The Times Educational Supplement*, 13 August.

Tilstone, C. (ed.) (1991) *Teaching Pupils with Severe Learning Difficulties*, London: David Fulton.

Tilstone, C. (1992) 'Severe Learning Difficulties', in Gulliford, R. and Upton, G. (eds) *Special Educational Needs*, London: Routledge.

Tomlinson, S. (1982) *A Sociology of Special Education*, London: Routledge and Kegan Paul.

Viinikka, S. (1993) 'Children looked after away from home: Some legal implications', in Batty, D. (ed.) *HIV Infection and Children in Need*, London: British Agencies for Adoption and Fostering.

Vlachou, A. and Barton, L. (1994) 'Inclusive Education: Teachers and the Changing Culture of Schooling', *British Journal of Special Education*, Vol. 21, No. 3, pp.105–11.

Wade, B. and Moore, M. (1993) *Experiencing Special Education: What young people with special educational needs can tell us*, Buckingham: Open University Press.

Williams, E. (1992) 'Wrath of Aids', *The Times Educational Supplement*, 27 November.
Wyman, R. (1986) *Multiply Handicapped Children*, London: Souvenir Press.

2 Visual impairment

Juliet Stone

What is visual impairment?

'Visual impairment' is a term used to describe any severe loss of sight, and includes a wide range of visual difficulties. For example, there may be a loss of functioning in the visual fields, perhaps in the peripheral field, leaving only the central part of the vision unimpaired. Another way in which vision may be affected is through a loss of clarity in the sight, so that nothing can be seen clearly. The impairment may be so severe that it results in a total lack of vision, though many people without sight prefer to refer to themselves as 'blind' individuals, rather than 'visually-impaired'.

As it is thought that 80 per cent of our information about the world is gained through sight, clearly any impairment of children's vision will have major implications. A visual impairment will affect development, education and the natural progression to increasing independence. It is important to note, however, that many children who are registered as blind do have some residual vision (Barraga and Morris, 1989). This, as well as adding to the children's quality of life, will help them in their development and learning. Even so, the implications for these children, their parents and teachers are severe, and the children are likely to face high levels of stress during their lives. These children will require in-depth programmes of intervention if they are to reach their full potential.

Children with partial sight will also have many problems, and these are perhaps not as well recognised by the layperson as are the problems which face the blind (Jose, 1983). There is a range of effects of partial sight which can cause children major difficulties. These difficulties will be different from those that face the totally blind, but these pupils will also require educational support if they are to make satisfactory progress. Some children's abilities to

21

use their vision will vary according to environmental factors, such as the weather. On a cloudy day, children with photophobia – a severe problem aggravated by strong light – will have no difficulty, whereas on a clear summer's day they may experience great visual difficulties. Another area of stress for children with low vision is that they fit neither into the role-model for the blind, nor to that for the fully-sighted. These children may well feel tempted to try to fit into the fully-sighted society, and pretend that they can see everything. This is not helpful to them, as they will miss out on so much experience and also the support that could be offered to them. On the other hand, children with low vision may become dispirited by their efforts to make sense of the world that they perceive through their eyes, and choose not to use what vision they do have effectively. Any intervention must take account of these differences in children with low vision, and the individuality of the impairment must be understood and accepted. In this way, the children will come to accept themselves and appreciate not only their difficulties, but also their strengths. Such intervention can be provided by educators, who, together with the parents, can assess the children's development, their strengths and their needs. Then – again together – parents and professionals can design and initiate educational programmes for the children.

The attitudes of society

The attitudes of those around them have a strong effect on the way children with visual impairments view themselves. Society appears to hold two main views of visual impairment and blindness. The first is that the world of blindness is one of darkness and despair, and that the person with a visual impairment is helpless and dependent, and needs pity and charity. The second view is one of utter admiration of the way blind people cope, and amazement at what blind individuals are able to achieve. There are media reports of blind people running in marathon races, climbing mountains, playing golf, and so on. There can be a feeling that what is true for these individuals can be true for all. But the vast majority of people with visual impairments do not fit into either of these two stereotypes, and they should be allowed to be themselves, just like individuals in the sighted population.

For the person with some residual vision, there seems to be no clear role-model, indeed most of us have little understanding of what is meant by 'partial sight'. The general public can be confused by the child who can ride a bicycle yet professes not to be able to see a book, and by the child who is able to read, yet not recognise a friend across the room. This lack in understanding of the particular difficulties of partial sight can lead to embarrassing and traumatic situations for children and young people. There may be occasions when they either have to try to explain their difficulties or accept the sometimes unkind comments that are made about them.

Everyone who is involved with visually-impaired people has a responsibility to raise public awareness. This can be achieved in various ways: for example, informative leaflets about visual impairment can be made available in schools, doctors' waiting rooms and other public places; open days in schools can be used for displays by the visually-impaired and for distributing information, and the use of the media could be extended.

The implications of a visual impairment

Visual impairment affects the development of the child in several ways. Lowenfeld (1971) observed the following effects: the limitation of experiences in terms of quality and quantity, and the restriction in the ability to move within the environment. Vision gives immediate access to the world around us. Visual impairment means that the world can only be experienced in a fragmentary way, through the other senses of hearing, touch, smell and taste. Visually-impaired children's development may follow a different path to that of fully-sighted children, or progress through different stages may be delayed (Fraiberg, 1977). It may be hard for such children to establish concepts without the information received through clear and accurate vision. However, Tobin (1979) found that, with appropriate intervention, young people with visual impairments do make up any developmental lag by the time they reach school leaving age, and the majority are on a par with fully-sighted children in terms of concept-formation.

A further implication of a visual impairment is that an enormous amount of effort and concentration is needed to cope with the business of daily living, such as dressing and undressing, eating or moving around. These activities can lead to a level of stress and fatigue that affects the functioning of the children.

The effect on the parents

One of the major implications of visual impairment in a child is the effect it has on the parents and the family. There is no doubt that the parents of visually-impaired children are faced with tremendous challenges. This is, of course, true for parents who have a child with any disability, but the parents of children who are born with a visual impairment are subject to specific stresses.

The early days of a baby's life with its parents are critical in the development of future relationships. Visual impairment may affect this development in one of two ways. Firstly, because many babies who are born with a visual impairment are premature, the care of the baby in a hospital intensive care unit may necessitate mother and baby being apart for the first few days or weeks. This separation may interfere with mother–baby bonding, which is regarded as crucial in the development of healthy social and emotional relationships. A second effect may be caused by the visual impairment itself, particularly if the baby is blind. Vision plays a crucial part in the establishment of the parent–baby relationship. Very few of us are able to pass a pram without looking into it and smiling into the eyes of the occupant inside, hoping to receive a smile or a gurgle in response. Wills (1978) talks about mothers and babies 'falling in love' with each other, and says that the eye contact between the two is a very important element in this. This falling in love can be seriously interrupted if the mother looks into expressionless, unseeing or unfocused eyes. The mother may not even be aware of what is making her feel so uncomfortable with her baby.

In addition, a delay in diagnosing a visual impairment brings its own tensions for the parents. Even today, with excellent medical care available in maternity hospitals, it may well be the parents who first identify the visual impairment and begin to wonder if anything is wrong with their baby's eyes. This can be a very worrying time. They ask themselves: 'Why is our baby reacting differently from other babies? Why is he or she not turning to look at things, not smiling at us?' This concern and stress can be compounded if medical personnel do not take the parents' concerns seriously or there is delay in the diagnosis. Any delay is worrying enough, but it also means that parents will have to wait for the support and guidance that will assist them in helping their baby.

The parents' progress to the acceptance of the baby's visual impairment will take different emotional paths and different periods of time for each individual family. Each family's response to the stress of the birth of a baby with a disability is 'normal' for them. This must be remembered and accepted by any professional who works with the family. Although some parents come to accept the impact of the disability through their own resources, others will need support and guidance if they are to learn how to cope with their own initial feelings, the attitudes of others and the management of their baby's development. The manner in which the diagnosis is first given, the immediacy of the support and counselling that is offered and the quality of the professionals who interact with the family at this crucial time will all have an impact on the parents, and therefore on the baby. It is also important to ensure that parents are given all the information which is available so that they can make an informed choice regarding the forms of support and the type of educational placement they want for their child.

As the child's life will be inextricably bound up with its parents, each stage of development will have an effect on the parents, and the reverse, of course, is also true. From the initial moves to independence, beginning with skills of feeding and toileting, to moving into education and on to college and employment, there will need to be close collaboration between the parents and professionals. Any intervention programme will need to work both directly with the child and with and through the parents. Their attitude to the programme will have a direct bearing on its success, and this needs to be remembered as we now consider the main stresses which children with a visual impairment may face.

In a brief summary such as this, it is impossible to do more than highlight the major effects that a visual impairment may have on the development of children. However, it is useful to consider the important stages that children pass through, and identify strategies which will enable learning to take place.

The early years

It is well accepted that the early years of children's lives are crucial to their future development (Bee, 1981). During this period the basis of future development and learning is established. A severe visual impairment will have implications for many aspects of their lives. Although each of these aspects – the physical, social, emotional, concept-development, and so on – are inter-related, the implications of visual impairment can be shown more clearly through considering each area separately.

Physical development

The impact of visual impairment on the physical development of children is great, as there are both direct and indirect influences at work. The direct influences of visual impairment mean that, with limited vision, it can be difficult for children to understand their bodies and how they work. So much of our understanding of our bodies, our posture, gait and movement comes through sight. We see our reflection in mirrors, we see other people in an upright position, and this information helps us to develop and maintain movement skills. However, parents can be shown how to help visually-impaired children learn about their bodies. For example, bells on ribbons can be tied round their ankles. The experience of the sound which results from movement of the feet will help the babies to learn about their limbs. The normal routines of the day offer many opportunities for making the babies aware of various parts of their bodies. Bathing, nappy changing and dressing times can be used by the carers to stroke, massage and move the little bodies. Through stroking the babies' limbs, each of the fingers and toes and the back of the legs, the babies can begin to understand their bodies. The advice of a physiotherapist can be enormously helpful (Chapman and Stone, 1988). Physiotherapists know how to encourage movement in young children and can advise parents on how to handle their children.

However, the indirect influences can be as great. Children learn about the environment through moving within it. Visual impairment does not mean that children will not be able to move. However, it does mean that they will not be motivated to move through seeing the exciting world around them, and it means that they will be very fearful of moving. Without clear vision, it is difficult to move freely and confidently in space. They will naturally be afraid of bumping into or tripping over obstacles. However, the adults around them must not discourage the children from exploring and moving within their environment. Bumps and bruises and a few tears are part of every child's life, and there may have to be more of these for the child with restricted vision. Of course, every effort must be made to ensure that the environment is safe, and the carers must support the child to make him or her feel secure enough to risk and endure minor injuries. It can be particularly hard for parents to do this, but preventing the child from moving at a young age will have implications for all future development (Norris et al., 1957).

Social and emotional development

Another major area of development which will be affected by a visual impairment is the social and emotional aspect. It has already been shown how restricted vision or blindness can interfere with establishment of mother–baby bonding through the lack of eye contact. However, babies also recognise their mothers through the sound of their voice or their individual smell, and mothers can be helped to interpret their babies' behaviour which shows this. For example, babies with little vision are likely to become very still when they sense their mother is approaching, so that they can gain as much information as possible from their sense of hearing. At the sound of mother's voice, they may make minuscule movements, such as moving their fingers or curling up their toes. Once mothers appreciate that this happens only as a response to them, they feel gratified and the relationship develops. However, if mothers are not helped to do this, the babies may well become the apathetic, non-responsive babies discussed by Wills (1978).

Much of our social behaviour is learned through imitation. Young children learn their social skills through watching others around them, and they practise these skills in play. Children with visual impairments will need to be shown these skills over and over again in order to learn them.

Language

Language is another area of development where the indirect influences of a visual impairment need to be ameliorated. A visual impairment, of itself, does not delay language development. However, if the young child does not see, the motivation to communicate will be restricted. Very young fully-sighted children communicate with the others around them because of their excitement at what they see. They use gesture to communicate, pointing to exciting objects, such as the movement of the family pet. Without the stimulation which vision provides, there may be little to talk about. The adults around the children will need to encourage the use of language by giving the children many and varied experiences and by using their own language to explain the world to the children. In addition, for language to develop, the young children will have to make good use of their listening skills. In order to do this, they need to be able to hear the every-day sounds around them – for example, the clock in the sitting room or the fridge in the kitchen. It is not helpful if the young child is constantly surrounded by background noise, such as that from a radio, television or tape recorder. These can have a place in the day-to-day routine of the child, but they do prevent the child from hearing and learning to understand other environmental sounds.

Other possible problems

Vision is the unifying sense, and without it, or with limited vision, the child may have difficulty making sense of the information which is perceived through the other senses. They may experience great stress while they are trying to get to grips with the complex and confusing world around them. This stress may be shown by the children withdrawing into themselves or displaying some odd behaviours, known as 'mannerisms', perhaps manifested as repetitive movements, such as rocking, either in a standing or sitting position, or twirling round and round; other examples include eye-poking or shaking their fingers in front of their eyes. These mannerisms are not necessarily evidence of stress, they may just be minor habits that the children have developed. However, whatever the cause, it is preferable if the cycle of behaviour can be broken, because it interferes with the child's learning, and the mannerisms themselves can be stigmatising. The first step in diverting the children from these behaviours is to discover the cause and to answer the question: What is the child doing immediately before he or she starts the particular mannerism? The mannerisms may start because the children are bored and understimulated. Conversely, the children may retreat into these behaviours because there is too much going on around them, or because they are being asked to do something that frightens or worries them. The behaviour cannot be prevented until the cause is known.

Young children with visual impairments can develop skills and reach satisfactory levels of achievement. Early intervention from professionals who have the sensitivity to work with families, and the necessary expertise in visual impairment and its effect on development, can be enormously helpful, providing support for the parents which will enable them to find a way to interact with the baby through cuddling, tickling and appropriate handling. The baby will then feel secure emotionally and be enabled to develop. Educational programmes can be initiated which will include activities to develop all the self-help skill areas, to encourage the child to explore and have fun, and develop independence. Many young children with visual impairments will benefit from a pre-school educational placement. This will give them the opportunity to develop social interaction with children of the same age and give them access to a whole new range of experiences and activities.

Educational placement

As the children near the age of 5, the question of educational placement arises. In the context of the general population, visual impairment is a minority disability. This affects the variety of educational placements available in any one region (RNIB, 1985). For example, there is unlikely to be a special school for visually-impaired children in the locality, except in the larger urban conurbations. This means that, if it is decided that a special school is the appropriate placement for an individual child, he or she will probably have to attend as a boarder. This can affect the decision of parents and local authorities, and will certainly place some stress on the child.

Educational placement may either be (a) in a special school for the visually-impaired, (b) within a resource centre at a mainstream school, or (c) the child may be placed individually in an integrated placement. There are advantages to the provision within a special school and that found in a mainstream placement, as well as disadvantages. The special school will be able to provide a setting where the pupil is fully understood by all members of staff, who will be trained and experienced in the education of visually-impaired children. The curriculum will be adapted for pupils with visual impairments. A wealth of equipment and technology will be available, and as all the pupils will be using one form of equipment or another, the individual children will not feel embarrassed at using theirs. There will be a multi-media approach, with material being available in large print, braille or audio form. The need to give access to the Special Curriculum will be understood by the staff, and the timetable will allow for mobility lessons or braille tuition. All the children will have visual impairments, so each will understand the other's problems; on the other hand, they will not make too many allowances on account of these problems. However, although the special schools do make efforts to mix with children from mainstream schools, there is little opportunity for day-to-day working and playing with fully-sighted children. This safe, secure environment may leave the pupils vulnerable once they leave school and enter the adult, sighted world.

Mainstream provision can take two forms. The resource centre will be based in a mainstream primary or secondary school. Most of the children from the locality who have visual impairments will attend the school and register with the appropriate age classes within it. They will be supported by the teachers in the resource centre, who will be trained and qualified teachers of the visually-impaired (Benton, 1982). These teachers will provide the resources and equipment that the pupils need, and support them in individual lessons where necessary, such as in science or physical education. The children will take their place alongside their fully-sighted peers and share in collaborative working with them. In addition, there will be other children with visual impairments with whom they can relate if they wish. However, in order to attend this school, the children with visual impairments will probably have had to travel for some distance, perhaps up to an hour in a taxi. This means that they have a very long and tiring day, and also that the children they work and play with at school will not necessarily be from their home locality. Loneliness and isolation may result.

The other example of mainstream provision – integrated placement – is where the child is entered into the local school and supported by visiting teachers of the visually-impaired. Here, the children with whom the visually-impaired child mixes at school will probably be from their own neighbourhood, and there is an opportunity for real relationships to be established. However, there is unlikely to be on-site expertise or provision of resources, and for most of the mainstream staff, this individual pupil will probably be the only visually-impaired child they have met.

Children with visual impairments differ from their peers in some of their educational needs. For those involved in making the decision about appropriate provision, the choice is between placing children with those with similar impairments in special schools, or placing them in ordinary schools, where their special needs will set them apart from other children. It is vital that the decision about placement is made with the child's best interests in mind, rather than for philosophical or local political reasons. The decision should not only be made with reference to the individual visual defect; there are other factors, such as the ability and personality of the individual children, which need to be taken into account (Stone, 1992). However, some general requirements for visually-impaired pupils must be considered before a placement decision can be made. These include access to the National Curriculum and all the other subjects which the fully-sighted child is taught, and access to the Special Curriculum, which includes the teaching of braille where necessary, education in mobility and personal living skills, and the

development of residual vision and good listening skills. Another requirement is that the children's social needs should be met, with opportunities for
social interaction with their peers, both visually-impaired and fully-sighted.
It is important that children are given the opportunity to mix with both these
groups of children. It can be very supportive to meet other children with
the same disability as oneself, as they really can appreciate the problems.
However, the opportunity to meet, work and play with fully-sighted children and young people is also important for the children we are considering.
Such social interactions will be very important for life outside school and for
future life.

Gaining access to the curriculum

Differing visual impairments present children with a variety of problems in
gaining access to the curriculum. The children who use braille will clearly
need specific tuition in braille and the provision of curriculum materials in
braille. However, for many pupils who are partially-sighted, the main
problem will be that the time taken to process information will be much
longer than for fully-sighted children. This means that visually-impaired
children have to work far harder and for much longer than their fully-
sighted peers to reach the same standard (Mason and Tobin, 1986). One
example of this is the child who has a visual field loss and so needs extra time
to copy from the blackboard: first, the words on the blackboard need to be
located, then the child has to find the correct place in the book on the desk,
and then relocate the work on the board. Another example concerns pupils
who, because of their visual difficulties, have a much slower reading speed.
The amount of work that they can get through is much less than the pupils
with full vision. Once teachers understand this, allowances can be made for
the children's work – not in quality, but in quantity. They can be given
smaller amounts of work which is equally as challenging as the work
expected of the fully-sighted pupils.

Much of the National Curriculum material is visual, which makes
concepts difficult for the visually-impaired pupil to grasp – for example, the
material used in mathematics includes many graphs and diagrams. Pupils
with visual field defects may take several minutes to scan the material, yet
the actual problems involved may be very simple and well within their ability.
The effort of looking at the material may cause the pupils much tension and
fatigue. The same is true for geography and many other subjects. However,
there are many strategies that can be used to help these children. The learning environment can be adapted to make it appropriate for the individual
child. The quality of lighting can be improved for the child with residual
vision. In addition, modified, enlarged or braille material can be provided. In
mainstream schools, where pupils with visual impairments are integrated,

academic and pastoral support can be made available by specialist teachers of the visually-impaired. These teachers can support the class and subject teachers in giving the pupils full access to the curriculum. The provision of suitable resources, especially technology, can give the pupils access to printed material and provide a multi-media approach to the learning situation. Special arrangements, such as extra time or the provision of someone to write on behalf of the pupils, can be made for examinations.

A further problem is that pupils may have a real struggle to manage practical tasks, such as science experiments, cooking and craft subjects. Support for pupils in these subjects can again be provided in mainstream schools by specialist teachers or by fully-sighted peers. Adapted equipment can also be helpful in many instances.

There may also be difficulties in the areas of physical education and games. Pupils with visual impairments may find these subjects very difficult, and will be unable to compete as equals with their fully-sighted peers. However, there are areas of the physical education curriculum where these pupils can excel. One young woman with a very severe visual impairment won her county's top award for gymnastics, and many such young people can achieve high standards in dance, athletics or swimming.

Stresses in adolescence

The period of adolescence and puberty can be a difficult time for both young people themselves and their parents. It is probable that a disability will exacerbate these difficulties, and this is certainly true for young people with visual impairments. Adolescence is a period when, for most young people, the struggle for their own independence begins. Young people want to make their own decisions, test the boundaries of authority and express their own individuality. It is also a time when peer pressure is at its greatest, and conforming to the peer norms in fashion, music, and so on becomes all-important.

The young person with a visual impairment is at a great disadvantage in many of these normal activities of adolescence. It is often at adolescence that the full impact of their impairment is felt, and the young people have to face the fact that they are visually-impaired for life. The emotional trauma that this causes frequently calls for a period of mourning for the lost or absent vision. Adults involved with these young children should ensure that counselling and emotional support is available should it be required.

The problem of restricted mobility for adolescents is a major cause of stress. If questioned, the young people state that their inability to drive a car is one of their major losses. However, apart from this, independent mobility will be difficult for many such adolescents. Unless they have had a full programme of mobility training, they will be dependent on fully-sighted people to take them out. This is bad for their self-esteem, and is also likely to restrict their social opportunities. As one young man said: 'I haven't finished my training yet and it's awful having to get my girlfriend to come and get me if we are going to a disco or something.' He added: 'It's even worse if I have to get Mum or Dad to take me – I'd rather not go.' The ability to form social relationships, to pursue employment, to follow leisure and recreational pursuits is affected by the difficulties of moving around in the environment. All young children should be assessed in terms of mobility on a regular basis, and any training needs identified. They can then meet adolescence with as much independence in mobility as possible.

There are other difficulties which the young person with a visual impairment must face. Adolescence is known as a time of inward vulnerability, and social situations can cause them enormous stress. One young lady said: 'When we're in the pub, I can't see what's going on and when the gang start laughing, I'm always afraid that it's at me!' In addition, visually-impaired adolescents miss the raised eyebrow and the meaningful gesture which is such a great part of social interactions. Young people are usually very concerned that their style of dress should fit the current trends in fashion. But adolescents who are severely visually-impaired may never have chosen clothes for themselves, or will have had their choice very much guided by adults, rather than their peers. They may be aware that their style of dress is inappropriate, but they don't get the necessary feedback or opportunity to allow them to modify their style. As difficult as it may be, adults involved with these adolescents must help them to be aware of the modern trends and allow them to follow them.

The social situation of eating can be yet another cause of stress for visually-impaired young people. Eating in a group situation when you can't see, or can't see clearly, is difficult. Some young people will always ask for the same meal, one they know they can cope with without exposing themselves to the risk of making a mess. If techniques of eating have been taught and encouraged in the early years, this difficulty can, to some extent, be prevented.

Peer approval is crucial at this stage in development, but young people with a visual impairment may be unaware of how to obtain it. They may be unaware of certain nuances of social behaviour, and can sometimes behave inappropriately.

As has been said, having a visual impairment can so easily lead to dependence on fully-sighted people. In this situation, it will be difficult for these adolescents to express their individuality. It will also be difficult for them to make decisions for themselves when carrying out those decisions involves seeking help from others. One way of preventing this is to develop the young person's self-esteem and confidence through overcoming challenges in the early years. If young people are experienced in problem-solving, coping with negative attitudes and surmounting obstacles, their feelings of self-worth will be established. In addition, personal counselling can help adolescents come to terms with their visual impairment and its implications for their future life, including the choice of career and issues surrounding marriage and personal relationships. Specific training can be given in the important areas of self-presentation skills, the art of conversation, the manner of dressing and the skills of eating appropriately. Expertise in these areas can add enormously to a young person's confidence and will stand them in good stead as they venture out from the protected atmosphere of school into the adult world.

Conclusion

Visual impairments and the stresses they bring can lead to a very dependent and passive existence for many children and young people. This chapter has tried to show that there are many strategies that can be adopted by both the involved adults and the children themselves which will allow them to lead a full and successful life. The human spirit thrives on overcoming challenges. Young people with visual impairments have an equal right to be allowed to feel the sense of achievement that this brings.

References

Barraga, N.C. and Morris, J.E. (1989) *Program to Develop Efficiency in Visual Functioning*, Louisville, Kentucky: American Printing House for the Blind.

Bee, H. (1981) *The Developing Child* (3rd edn), London: Harper International.

Benton, S. (1982) 'Supporting Visually Handicapped Children in Ordinary Schools', University of Birmingham, unpublished dissertation.

Chapman, E.K. and Stone, J.M. (1988) *The Visually Handicapped Child in Your Classroom*, London: Cassell.

Fraiberg, S. (1977) *Insights From the Blind*, London: Souvenir Press.

Jose, R. (1983) *Understanding Low Vision*, New York: American Foundation for the Blind.

Lowenfeld, B. (1971) *Our Blind Children*, Springfield, Illinois: Charles Thomas.

Mason, H. and Tobin, M.J. (1986) 'Speed of Information Processing and the Visually Handicapped Child', *British Journal of Special Education*, Vol. 13, No. 2.

Norris, M., Spaulding, P.J. and Brodie, F.H. (1957) *Blindness in Children*, Chicago, Illinois: University of Chicago Press.

RNIB (Royal National Institute for the Blind) (1985) *Second Demographic Study: Visually-Handicapped Children*, London: Royal National Institute for the Blind.

Stone, J.M. (1992) 'Advisory Services for the Visually Impaired – A National Provision?', *British Journal of Visual Impairment*, Autumn.

Tobin, M.J. (1979) *A longitudinal study of blind and partially sighted children in special schools in England and Wales*, Birmingham: Research Centre for the Visually Handicapped.

Wills, D. (1978) 'Work with Mothers of Young Blind Children', *Occasional Papers*, Vol. 2, No. 2, pp.32–8.

Further reading

Readers who wish more information about children with visual impairments are referred to the following books.

Best, A.B. (1992) *Teaching Children with Visual Impairments*, Milton Keynes: Open University.

Chapman, E.K. and Stone, J.M. (1988) *The Visually Handicapped Child in Your Classroom*, London: Cassell.

In addition, a large number of informative booklets are readily available from the Royal National Institute for the Blind, 224 Great Portland Street, London N1 6AA.

3 Hearing impairment

Rachel Godfrey and Christa Schreiber-Kounine

Introduction

One in three children present with a *conductive hearing loss* during their childhood. 'Conductive hearing loss' is defined here as a non-permanent malfunction of the middle ear, often caused by what is generally known as 'glue-ear'. This 'glue', a sticky fluid in the ear, prevents appropriate sound conduction and therefore causes distortion in the perception of sound. The high prevalence of glue-ear in young children is partly due to the anatomy of their ears and nose, and particularly the Eustachian tubes, making the drainage of excess fluid caused by colds and/or allergies difficult.

Sensorineural hearing loss is found in 1 per cent of children, and is defined here as permanent damage to the auditory nerve. This damage is irreversible, and the resultant hearing loss can be of varying degrees, ranging from mild to moderate to profound. Profound hearing loss is often synonymous with the term 'deaf', but in this chapter we will use the term 'hearing impairment' as an all-embracing term for any degree of hearing loss.

Hearing loss can take many different forms, sometimes affecting only high- or low-frequency sounds. The degree and nature of hearing loss determines to a great extent the acquisition of oral language, as does the gain in sound/speech perception achieved through amplification with hearing aids. Other contributing factors are the general level of intelligence and possible additional impairments.

The most worrying feature of any hearing impairment – permanent or temporary – for a hearing family is the negative effect it may have on the child's ability to understand and produce oral language. This in turn may cause all sorts of stresses, both for the child and the family, which will be elaborated in the following sections.

35

Stress and coping

Hearing-impaired children and their families may be referred to clinical child psychologists by consultants in audiological medicine at two quite distinct stages of their management:

1   shortly after the diagnosis, especially if the news seems to have had a particularly distressing effect on the family;
2   when a hearing-impaired child presents with a problem affecting either their family or schooling (or both).

Both kinds of referral suggest a broadening of the focus, from the individual child to the family in which the child lives.

All families can expect to experience normative developmental crises, such as the birth of their first child, children reaching adolescence and the 'empty nest' syndrome, each having in common a redefinition of roles within the couple or family system (Carter and McGoldrick, 1989). The birth of a hearing-impaired child can be conceptualised as an idiosyncratic or non-normative stressor, adding to and possibly exacerbating the normative stresses. The diagnosis of a hearing impairment can easily lead to a severe temporary upheaval within the family, with some families requiring focused, short-term professional intervention, whilst others cope well alone. The question that arises is: what enables some families to cope better than others?

A number of different stress and coping models have been proposed (for a recent review see Beresford, 1994), some of which focus on the individual (Lazarus and Folkman, 1984) and others on the family (Patterson and McCubbin, 1983), but their central tenets are that potential stressors undergo an *appraisal*, and that they mobilise *resources*.

The appraisal determines whether the potential stressor is perceived as a threat/challenge, or as benign or even irrelevant. Resources include personal ones, such as personality characteristics, cognitions, physical health and skills, on the one hand and socio-ecological ones, such as financial resources and social and professional networks, on the other. The family's appraisal of the stressor (for example, hearing impairment) is influenced by their resources and will influence these in turn (see Figure 3.1 for a simplified model of stress and coping).

This recursive process could be defined as 'stress' (Gaudet and Powers, 1989), which may be particularly challenging if the family is unable to use existing resources, and/or has few resources available to them, or if the family perceives their resources as inadequate in relation to the stressor. In families with an impaired child, a pile-up of stressors is often found. For

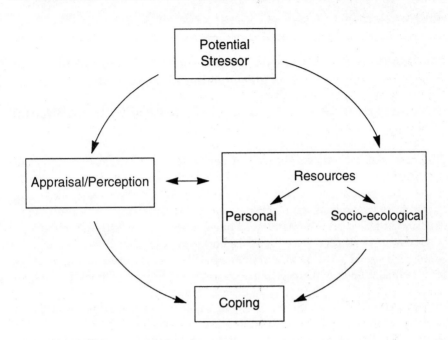

Figure 3.1 Stress and coping model

these families, coping involves use of both existing and new resources (for example, teachers of the deaf, hearing aids), the adequacy of which will again be influenced by (and influence) their perception of the stressor, resulting eventually in some form of adaptation.

Stress and coping research has shown that the severity of an impairment does not correlate with the severity of stress created for a family. This strongly suggests that the family's perceptions both of stressors upon them and of their resources have a mediating influence on adaptation, which in turn affects how the hearing-impaired child (and the siblings) adapt. Supporting evidence for this view is the finding that deaf children of deaf parents present with less behavioural and emotional problems than hearing-impaired children of hearing parents, as deaf parents will normally perceive the diagnosis of hearing impairment as much less challenging and traumatic than hearing parents.

As the child and family develop and milestones have to be negotiated, further stressors from within the child, the family and/or the environment may pose additional challenges for both child and family, creating vulnerbility but not necessarily dysfunction. These potential stressors will be outlined in the following sections.

Sensorineural hearing loss

The discussion of potential stressors below is by no means exhaustive, but reflects the problems most commonly encountered in clinical practice.

Potential stressors for pre-school children with sensorineural hearing loss

Behavioural difficulties   Young children often express their feelings and experiences in their behaviour, and so-called 'behavioural problems' may be the first sign of stress caused by a variety of factors. An as yet undetected hearing loss manifests itself through apparent non-compliance with verbal instructions delivered by parents or nursery staff. The children may present with outbursts of seemingly inexplicable aggression – such as lashing out at their peers – or with total withdrawal. These behaviours result from the children's difficulty in decoding verbal information and their inability to respond verbally, leading to dual frustration: lack of understanding of what is expected of them and what is going on in the world around them, and frustration at not being able to make themselves understood. Other means of communication, such as hitting and pushing, are used to compensate for the lack of verbal communication.

Once the diagnosis of hearing impairment has been made and appropriate amplification provided, a reduction in 'behavioural problems' may occur. However, more often than not, families go through a period of distress immediately after the diagnosis. It poses a point of crisis and increased vulnerability, as parents experience loss: loss of the 'perfect child' and of perfect hearing ability in their child. This causes feelings of shock and disbelief, followed by sadness, which may be projected inwards as guilt and outwards as anger. The wish to protect the child from further mishaps may lead to overprotectiveness, reducing opportunities for the child to acquire new skills (for example, riding a bike). This overprotectiveness may in turn lead to rebellious behaviour on the part of the child. Similarly, parents, feeling compelled to compensate for the loss, may find it difficult to set clear boundaries and to implement rules, perceiving these as too punitive. Inconsistent rules and fluctuating boundaries are difficult for young children to deal with, and even more difficult for hearing-impaired children, invariably leading to behavioural problems.

Communication problems   As the parents come to terms with the diagnosis of a sensorineural hearing loss, they will reflect upon their way of communicating with their hearing-impaired child, often leading to them feeling temporarily de-skilled, tense and confused.

Parents are, on the whole, brilliant communicators, fine-tuning their speech to their child's by simplifying what they say and clarifying meaning through repetition of key words and by paraphrasing new words. Communication happens within the natural context of interactions as a two-way process. The child takes the initiative, whilst the adult role is to structure the task by prompting, making suggestions and providing feedback. In other words, the parent facilitates communication rather than teaching it.

In interactions with hearing-impaired children, parents' natural communication skills are often temporarily lost due to anxiety and insecurity. Interactions between the parent and hearing-impaired child become more directive, with the child being asked to attend to the adults and adapt to their instructions, rather than vice versa. This means that hearing impairment does not merely restrict what the child can hear, but it may also disrupt some of the normal social interactive processes which lay the foundations of communication.

Sleep difficulties   Sleep difficulties are fairly common in young children, with 20 per cent of 1–2-year-olds and 14 per cent of 3-year-olds presenting with night waking. A similar proportion of 3-year-olds present with 'settling' (or 'going-to-bed') problems. Among hearing-impaired children, the prevalence rates are even higher. There may be a number of reasons for sleep difficulties, with fear of darkness being very common among young children. Whilst hearing children can be reassured of their parents' presence by being able to hear them move around, talk and listen to the radio or television, hearing-impaired children need reassurance through visual or physical contact.

Potential stressors for school-age children with sensorineural hearing loss

Acceptance   When a child approaches school age, it is an important milestone for any family, as it involves choosing the 'right' school for one's child on the one hand, and the process of 'letting go' on the other. The parents of a hearing-impaired child are faced with additional options of school placement, such as partially-hearing units and schools for the deaf – options that they would not have considered normally, highlighting the reality of the loss and probably re-evoking the process of grieving. Often parents are taken aback by the intensity of their feelings of sadness and loss, and professional or social support is much more scarce than after the initial diagnosis.

The choice of school will depend upon many different factors: the nature and severity of the hearing loss, the gain in auditory perception achieved through amplification, the communicative and intellectual abilities of the child, and the preference of the parents.

Peer-groups: Different or the same?   Whilst partially-hearing units (PHUs) promote integration, they may not always provide an appropriate peer-group for the hearing-impaired child to find like-minded friends and role-models. The stronger the emphasis on integration and on 'being the same', either at school or at home, the more any difference in the ability to hear and communicate will be felt. This creates considerable tension in the hearing-impaired youngster which may be expressed in a number of ways (for example, through school-refusal, conduct disorder, social phobias, etc.). A recent study by Hindley et al. (1994) suggests a higher prevalence of psychiatric disorders amongst hearing-impaired children at PHUs in comparison to those at deaf schools. It is particularly stressful for the hearing-impaired child if parents and teachers disagree with each other's approach to communication. The tension created by this conflict of opinions is often mirrored in behaviour problems.

Schools for the deaf are more likely to provide a peer-group and possible role-models, but may create a worrying physical and emotional distance between the hearing-impaired child and his or her family. Often distances are too great to be travelled daily, meaning that the hearing-impaired child will have to board at school. Furthermore, the school provides a 'deaf culture' to which the hearing have little access. Some special schools may also be limited in the educational qualifications they can offer.

Specific learning and communication difficulties   During the primary school years, additional difficulties such as specific learning difficulties and/or communication problems may surface, but these may not be fully investigated or diagnosed, owing to the often low expectations of a hearing-impaired child's reading attainment and oral language. But just as some hearing children suffer from language disorders or specific reading retardation, so can a hearing loss be complicated by these additional problems. Failure to recognise these specific problems will cause additional stress for the child and family, potentially leading to frustration, loss of motivation, self-image problems or conflict within the family.

Communication   As the child grows older, language becomes more abstract and sophisticated. Depending on the severity of the hearing loss, the development of abstract verbal language may not only be slower but severely restricted, limiting the child's ability to express thoughts and feelings verbally as well as to negotiate relationships. Misunderstandings occur easily between human beings and are difficult to clear up without high-level communication skills. Different forms of communication (for example, sign language) may need to be considered to enable the hearing-impaired youngster to acquire communication skills that gradually but steadily increase in complexity.

Self-esteem   Adolescence imposes further changes on the family's lifestyle. Roles within the family have to be redefined, with the parents having to give up some of their authority and the adolescents gaining in independence. Adolescents often become introspective and self-critical, and for the hearing-impaired teenager, this often means facing the implications of his or her impairment. Personal attractiveness *vis-à-vis* the opposite or same sex is questioned, as is the ability to gain professional qualifications and financial independence. Peer-group pressure to conform is high, often exacerbated through bullying, and role-models may be scarce, especially at partially-hearing units. Conflicts between deaf culture and hearing culture and different communication approaches used by parents and adolescents may arise, all of which constitute potential stressors for the hearing-impaired adolescent. This in turn may reinforce the parents in their belief that the adolescent still needs to be protected. An interactive process can occur, where low parental or teacher expectations lead to feelings of inadequacy, which results in the adolescent either not trying, or performing poorly, again leading to low expectations, and so on. Low self-esteem and even depression may follow.

Interestingly, the self-image of hearing-impaired adolescents at deaf schools seems better than that of hearing-impaired teenagers at PHUs, probably because of increased opportunities for positive identification with peers and deaf role-models and reduced victimisation at deaf schools.

Tinnitus   Tinnitus may be described as the perception of a sound or sounds (often a buzzing, whistling or ringing type of noise) in the absence of any auditory stimulation. Tinnitus affects 1 in 3 hearing-impaired children. However, it does not pose a particular problem to all children who present with it.

Tinnitus is usually only perceived as a problem or as an interference with normal every-day life when importance is attached to the sound, usually in terms of negative associations related to the noise. For instance, the noise may be viewed as being evidence of an as yet undiscovered illness or the development of madness, or the sufferer may become distressed at the thought of being denied the sound of 'silence'. As yet, these issues have not been explored in any great depth in children, but from the small amount of evidence available, their responses have been found to be similar to those of adults. If the tinnitus becomes the person's main focus of attention, it may contribute towards the onset of sleep disorders and may also cause lack of concentration on daily activities, including both schoolwork and social and leisure pursuits. In the most severe cases, the distress felt may be enough to cause depression.

For many young children, tinnitus does not pose a particular problem, probably because they do not remember life without these internal noises, and therefore perceive them as 'normal' and non-threatening. As stress is known to increase the perception of tinnitus as an 'annoyance', young children who are not anxious about their tinnitus and who have no negative associations attached to it are not troubled by it. School-age children, and in particular teenagers, seem far more worried about their tinnitus, and often attach to it some of the negative connotations previously described. This gives significance to the condition, which therefore commands attention, and the perception of the noises increases. Other anxieties felt by the older hearing-impaired child – such as feelings of being 'different', coming to terms with the permanence of his or her disability, and perhaps struggling to keep up in a mainstream school – all seem to increase the perception of tinnitus as a negative stressor and therefore maintain it in the forefront of the child's mind.

Conductive hearing loss

Many of the difficulties commonly experienced by children with a sensori-neural hearing loss and their families are also highly relevant to children with a conductive hearing loss. These include behavioural problems, communication difficulties, peer-group relationship difficulties and sleep disorders, as well as specific learning difficulties, which have already been discussed.

However, some other problems are fairly unique to children with conductive hearing losses and merit separate discussion.

Potential stressors for pre-school children with conductive hearing loss

Listening skills   Whilst it is generally acknowledged that children with severe to profound hearing losses will need to be taught how to listen, this is often overlooked in children with conductive – and therefore often less severe – hearing loss. They also have considerable difficulty in distinguishing important environmental noises such as speech sounds from other sounds such as chairs being moved in the classroom. This may subject the child to a continuous cacophony of noise, and the child may not know which sounds to attend to and which to ignore. This, in conjunction with their naturally limited ability to concentrate for long periods, results in fluctuating attention to the task at hand. This means that their listening skills are usually delayed in comparison with those of their peers.

Language   These children find the perception of language difficult because of the fluctuating and distorted nature of the auditory input they receive. This may have a detrimental effect not only on their understanding of language, but also on their clarity of speech and expressive language skills.

Potential stressors for school-age children with conductive hearing loss

Behavioural consequences of conductive hearing loss It is known from experience with hearing children that behaviour, social adjustment and learning are all interdependent. For instance, unhappy and maladjusted children or those who come from dysfunctional home environments often fail to learn. Although there is little research on the effects of a recurrent conductive hearing loss on children's behaviour and adjustment, it seems that, owing to the associated communication difficulties, they may be perceived as unwilling or slow to learn. Bax et al. (1983) found that children with middle ear infections had more temper tantrums and were more likely to be difficult to manage than children without these problems. Other studies have suggested conductive hearing loss may lead to a shy, listless and withdrawn personality (Rapin, 1979). These children are also likely to become frustrated and aggressive. Children with conductive hearing loss may have a large discrepancy between their verbal and non-verbal intellectual abilities, their verbal functioning and development being held back as a result of their recurrent middle ear infections. If this discrepancy in abilities is not detected and addressed at school, the children may begin to feel that they fail at most of the tasks they attempt. Over time, this may lead to a lowering of self-esteem and withdrawal on one hand, or alternatively, the child may become frustrated and behaviour problems may develop, either as an outlet for their frustration or as an attempt to divert attention away from their schoolwork.

Conductive hearing loss and educational achievement It is clear that early hearing loss will cause disruption to speech and language acquisition, which will in turn affect the child's learning at school. The question that needs to be asked is whether the school difficulties are a *result* of delayed language development, which in turn gives rise to reading and writing difficulties, because language is the main medium required for learning within a primary school classroom.

Sak and Ruben (1981) conducted a study whereby they administered the Wechsler Intelligence Scale for Children – Revised (WISC–R) to two groups of children: those with histories of early conductive hearing losses and their hearing siblings. WISC–R is an intelligence test tapping a wide range of cognitive skills in verbal and non-verbal areas of functioning. The non-verbal tests revealed no significant differences between the two groups. However, large differences were noticed on the verbal tests which require good expressive language skills. It can be seen, therefore, that children experience some pervasive effects of their early conductive hearing losses that affect their learning at a later stage. If the conductive hearing loss resolves itself, these difficulties are likely to be overcome and the children should be able to catch up with their peers in terms of their overall school performance. However, if the middle ear disease is chronic, a study by Kaplan et al. (1973) shows that the sufferers have much lower achievement levels in reading, mathematics and language. The root of these learning difficulties may lie in poor listening skills. As classrooms are often noisy places, a child with even a minor hearing loss can suffer from lack of concentration or attention, especially when there are several different auditory stimuli competing for attention.

Variable performance in schoolwork   It is thought that the fluctuating nature of conductive hearing loss makes it very difficult for the sufferer to compensate for it, and that this hinders progress at school. This intermittent hearing loss can confuse children at a critical time in their development, whereas a mild but constant hearing loss may not have such an adverse effect. At times when the children's hearing is poor, they are unable to learn the contrasting sounds of speech. At times when they are able to hear, instead of 'catching up' lost ground, they can become confused as they may not be able to find a match for the sounds they hear in their memory. This will adversely affect the acquisition of complex words and sentence structures which are dependent on the child's ability to decode and encode the sounds of speech.

Assessment

Within a specialised paediatric unit for speech, language and hearing problems, children with any of the aforementioned psychological difficulties associated with the different types of hearing impairments may be referred to the clinical psychologist.

In order to ascertain the nature and degree of the problem, as well as to identify and define the positive coping strategies the child and his or her family already have at their disposal (or where these may have broken down), a thorough and comprehensive assessment is required. Only through this procedure is it possible to implement an appropriate treatment programme that will enable the child and family to 'cope' with the stresses of their problem.

Why do we assess?

The purpose of any type of assessment is to build a complex picture of a child and his or her specific difficulties or problems within the context of his or her own environment, including the child's family and school/nursery system. It is essential to gather comprehensive life-history information, to enable the current behaviour of the child to be placed in the context of his or her past experiences.

As well as collecting a detailed case history from the child, parents and any other relevant source (for example, a schoolteacher), a comprehensive analysis of the current presenting problems should be carried out.

A framework for taking a comprehensive personal history

Family history   It is useful to construct a family tree as a basis for eliciting answers to the following questions:

- Who does the family consist of?
- Who lives at home?
- Who is responsible for the care of the child?
- What are the sibling relationships?
- Is there a history of similar problems in other family members?

Medical history   Ask about previous illnesses, operations, allergies, etc.

Developmental history/milestones

- Were there any ante-, peri- or post-natal problems?
- At what age did the child first sit, walk, talk, etc.?
- Have there been any previous developmental concerns?

Social/peer relationships

- Does the child have appropriate relationships?
- Investigate the nature of these relationships.

Schooling/education

- Is the child well settled and integrated at school?
- What is the child's level of achievement?
- What is the child's concentration/attention span like?
- Are there any other specific concerns about school?

General behaviour

- Is the child generally co-operative and even-tempered, or aggressive, or shy?
- Investigate the child's personality traits – these should generally be observable.

Sleep

- Does the child have a regular sleep pattern?
- Are there sleep problems? If so, investigate the cause and nature of them.

Feeding/eating behaviour

- Does the child eat well?
- Is the child a fussy eater?
- Is there evidence of any eating disorder? If so, investigate it.

Toileting

- Was the child dry/clean at an appropriate age?
- Were there any difficulties with toilet training?
- Is there an existing problem of enuresis or encopresis?

Finally, investigate any behavioural, social or emotional problems or learning difficulties not previously discussed.

A framework for gathering information about the presenting problem

The following framework is useful in gathering a history of the presenting problem. Generally, it is preferable for the historical perspective to be gathered from more than one source. This enables the clinician to cross-check the validity and accuracy of the information obtained. The structure of the interview can be divided into four steps.

Step 1 – What is the problem?   Answers to the following questions should be obtained:

- What does the child perceive the problem to be? Is this the same as the problem perceived by the parents?
- Does the problem involve a physical or verbal behaviour that is observable, or is it a covert problem?
- Does it involve a cognitive or imagined event?
- Is it a physical sensation such as fatigue, muscle tension, pain, etc.?
- What is the frequency of the problem?
- What is the current duration of the problem? This is likely to be more relevant where the problem involves a chain or sequence of behaviours – for example, loss of temper or concentration difficulties in the classroom, etc.

Step 2 – What does the child think causes the problem?   This step helps the child and parent to attribute the cause of problem behaviour to some triggering event or particular person. It is important to ascertain whether the cause of the problem is seen to be outside the child's control, their responsibility entirely, or a mixture of internal and external causation factors.

Step 3 – Behavioural analysis   Under what circumstances and conditions does the problem behaviour occur?

- When does it occur at its highest and lowest frequency?
- What else is the child doing when it occurs?
- Are the high and low occurrence rates related to any particular time of day or certain event?
- What events occur immediately prior to the problem behaviour or seem to elicit it? These antecedents may be overt (for example, locations, activities, external events), or they may be covert (for example, thoughts, images, physical sensations, and so on).
- What are the consequences for the child of the occurrence of the problem behaviour? Are these outcomes positive or negative for the child?

Step 4 – What is the history of the presenting problem?

- What specific events or circumstances are associated with the first occurrence of the problem behaviour?
- Has the frequency, duration and intensity of the problem changed over time?
- What attempts has the child made to change the frequency of the problem behaviour?

Behavioural formulation

The behavioural formulation summarises and integrates the data of the behavioural analysis above, and attempts to explain the acquisition and maintenance of the presenting complaint(s) in terms of learning principles. Ideally, the formulation should be capable of predicting a subject's behaviour in specified situations and provide testable hypotheses. It may be described in terms of the predisposing, precipitating and maintaining factors surrounding a behaviour, where predisposing factors are the initial cause of the behaviour in the past, precipitating factors are the current causes of the behaviour in the present, whilst maintaining factors ensure the behaviour carries on in the future.

Clinical experimentation

It may be necessary to obtain additional information to test hypotheses drawn from the formulation of the problem if the child presents with learning difficulties. This extra information is usually gathered through the process of formal psychometric assessment.

Formal psychometric assessment

The following is a brief description of the different psychometric testing instruments most frequently used in the assessment of hearing-impaired children, together with some guidelines as to their value in compiling a profile of a child's abilities across the various areas of cognitive functioning.

The Wechsler Intelligence Scale for Children (WISC–III UK)

The WISC–III UK is a clinical instrument used for assessing the intellectual ability of children in the 6-year to 16-year-11-month age range. It is an individually administered test consisting of a verbal and a performance (or non-verbal) scale, each composed of several subtests which measure different factors of intelligence. Three composite scores are obtained – the Verbal, Performance and Full Scale IQs – which give estimates of an individual's intellectual abilities. Wechsler viewed intelligence 'not as a particular ability but as an aggregate and global entity', therefore the WISC–III UK subtests have been chosen to tap various differing mental abilities, which together give an indication of a child's overall intellectual functioning.

Although intelligence can be conceptualised as being a 'global' entity, it does not follow that the abilities it comprises will all be equally well developed in any one individual. Most 'normal' children have peaks and troughs in their scores on the various tests, showing that they develop their cognitive skills in different ways and have varying patterns of cognitive strengths and needs.

The WISC–III UK does not cover *all* aspects of an individual's intelligence. Therefore the results must be used in conjunction with information on the child's traits and attitudes – including such attributes as anxiety, perseverance, impulsiveness, planning and goal awareness – all of which influence a child's overall performance – to come to a conclusion.

This instrument is immensely useful in identifying the patterns of strengths and needs in a child. However, its use with the hearing-impaired child is often somewhat limited, as firstly, it has not been standardised on the deaf population and has only been administered to a very small sample of deaf children, and secondly, even the performance subtests are constructed in such a way that the instructions are presented verbally, so these tests are biased against the child with limited language due to hearing impairment.

Where no alternative non-verbal IQ tests are available, the instructions for the performance subtests may be modelled, and the results will at least give a rough indication of the hearing-impaired child's abilities. The verbal scale is rarely useful or possible to administer with children whose language development is delayed due to a hearing impairment. With older deaf children or those with good language development, it may be attempted, although it may be necessary to have a sign interpreter in the room to aid the smooth running of the session.

The scores should always be interpreted very cautiously when standard administration procedures are modified for a special population. For example, the 'digit span' subtest is designed to look at short-term memory ability through a series of orally presented number sequences which the child repeats verbatim. If this subtest is administered in sign language, it may modify the construct being measured – it may tap visual rather than auditory memory – as well as possibly affecting the difficulty of the task.

The Wechsler Pre-school and Primary Scale of Intelligence – Revised (WPPSI–R UK)

The rationale behind the WPPSI–R UK is similar to the WISC–III UK, the difference being that it has been devised to test the intelligence of children aged from 3 years to 7 years 3 months. With the same premise that intelligence is globally rather than discretely defined, the WPPSI–R UK taps the individual young child's different aspects of intelligence through various tasks. The composite score of a child's performance on these tasks indicates the individual's ability to understand and cope with their environment.

As the behavioural repertoire of younger children differs markedly from those aged 6 and over – which is especially true for those children with impaired communication skills – different tests are required to measure their cognitive abilities.

British Ability Scales (BAS)

The BAS comprises a comprehensive intelligence test battery, developed with the aim of providing the tester with more flexibility than many other tests. There are many different scales to choose from, depending on the individual assessment need, most of which have been standardised over a wide age range (2 to 17 years). It has been developed especially for children, rather than being adapted from an adult version. As well as ability and developmental scales, the BAS includes scholastic attainment scales providing valuable information about discrepancies between attainment and ability. Although it is possible to calculate global IQ scores, the BAS also allows testing to be tailored to individual needs. The user can generate, test and expand hypotheses regarding a child's relative strengths and needs across various ability areas. The BAS can be used to identify children with various types of learning difficulties, and can help the user identify appropriate learning objectives and methods of achieving these. The advantage for the hearing-impaired child is that it is possible to select appropriate non-verbal tests without compromising the validity of the instrument by not administering the entire test.

Snijders-Oomen Non-Verbal Intelligence Scale (SON 2 1/2–7)

The SON 2 1/2–7 is one of the few intelligence tests available in this country specifically normed on deaf children. It also incorporates norms for hearing children. The instructions can easily be mimed so as not to disadvantage children with poor oral/aural communication skills.

The test consists of five subscales: SORTING, COMBINATION, MOSAIC, COPYING and MEMORY, looking at concept-formation, visual–spatial abilities, visual–motor co-ordination, fine motor control and visual memory. Both Mental Age and IQ scores can be computed. The test is appealing to young children as it demands less time and therefore less concentration on the part of the child than the WPPSI–R UK, and in our experience correlates highly with both Wechsler tests.

Hiskey-Nebraska Test of Learning Aptitude

The Hiskey-Nebraska Test of Learning Aptitude was designed to address the need for a non-verbal intelligence test normed on the deaf population. It can be used with children aged between 3 and 16 years. The instructions can be mimed, which requires prior practice. The test consists of 12 subtests, assessing visual memory, visual–spatial skills, visual–motor co-ordination, non-verbal reasoning, visual attention span and concept-formation. The subtests used depend upon the child's age. An overall score of Learning Aptitude is computed, similar to that of a Mental Age score. IQ scores can be obtained for hearing children but not for those who are hearing-impaired, making this test somewhat difficult to compare with other standardised tests.

Neale Analysis of Reading Ability

The Neale Analysis of Reading Ability is structured as an interaction between the child who is reading and the tester, who listens. It is suitable for measuring the reading ability of most children between the ages of 6 and 12 years. The test material is presented to the child as a book, which contains a series of graded narrative passages. Each one is constructed to contain a set amount of words and has a central storyline. To set the scene of the story, each passage is accompanied by a picture.

Reading accuracy is assessed by recording the errors made by the child. Comprehension is assessed through questions which are administered to the child after the oral reading of each passage. Immediate recall of the main concepts presented in the narrative is tested, as well as the sequence of events and some limited inference.

There are two parallel versions of this test, for which standardised scores are provided in terms of percentile ranks, and Reading Ages for Accuracy, Reading Rate and Comprehension.

Supplementary diagnostic tests are provided so that the tester is able to look at performance on individual component reading skills.

This test can only be administered to children with the necessary oral/aural communication skills.

Schonell Graded Word Spelling Test

There are two parallel versions of the Schonell Graded Word Spelling Test, each looking at spelling attainment in the 5- to 15-year-old age range. Each of the words to be written is first dictated by the tester, then embedded in an explanatory sentence, and then dictated again. From the total number of correctly spelled words, the Spelling Age of the child can be calculated, as well as the Spelling Quotient, which is an estimate of a pupil's spelling attainments in comparison with his or her chronological age. However, this test is often of limited usefulness for those children with little oral/aural language due to a hearing impairment.

Treatment

Theoretical overview of approaches to treatment

The four main treatment approaches used most commonly in working with hearing-impaired children are outlined below.

Behaviour therapy Behaviour therapy uses the principles of behaviour modification based on learning theory. It concerns itself with a patient's manifest or overt behaviours, which are more easily quantifiable than his or her covert ones. It seeks to avoid consideration of less conscious elements of a person's experience, and instead concentrates on the correction of overt maladaptive behaviours which have been acquired through past experiences. It is especially effective for monosymptomatic phobias and behaviour problems.

Cognitive behaviour therapy   Cognitive behavioural methods are directly concerned with the relationship between a patient's thoughts and feelings. Treatment is generally based in the present, and assumes that the main goal of therapy is for patients to bring about the changes in their life that they desire. Problem-solving is an important part of this therapy. The patient is given explanations about the components of the therapy and encouraged to form a collaborative team with the therapist, working together to solve dilemmas and plan strategies to deal with clearly-identified problems. The central principle of cognitive behavioural assessment is that individuals' behaviour is determined by their interpretation of their situation.

Family therapy   Family therapy is a therapeutic approach based on systems theory, which postulates that the behaviour of one part of the system, for example one family member, invariably impacts on other parts of the system. Although only one family member may present with a symptom, this symptom can often serve a function within the family. Family interactions are analysed, and interventions are directed at changing the pattern of interactions. Depending on the model used, these interventions might be very direct and pragmatic or take the form of theoretical interpretations.

Counselling   Counselling may be viewed in a variety of ways. On the one hand it may be seen as a chance for a person to share his or her thoughts and feelings about a particular event or set of circumstances he or she is finding hard to deal with. Alternatively, the counsellor may be viewed as a 'sounding board' for testing options or new ways of tackling a problem. It can provide a person with time and space to think through the pros and cons of difficult decisions in a safe and supportive environment. People often come to counselling following a traumatic event (such as their child being diagnosed with a hearing impairment). It gives them a chance to share their thoughts and feelings and gradually come to terms with the situation. The main aim of counselling is not to 'solve' the problem, but to help the person confront his or her fears and come to an equilibrium whereby he or she can live more easily with the difficulty.

Practical application of treatment approaches

Potential stressors for the hearing-impaired child and his or her family have been described in some detail. Psychological assessment procedures aimed at identifying the nature and impact of the stressor have also been outlined. Psychological intervention will be determined by the outcome of this assessment process, and therefore individually tailored to the child's and family's needs using the stress and coping model discussed earlier (see pages 36–7). The focus for the professional in contact with a family of a hearing-impaired child will be:

- how the family *perceives* the stressful event;
- which *resources* are available to the family.

Perceptions include religious and other beliefs, family myths, perceived control over events and problem-solving ability. Such beliefs, attitudes and skills are all aspects of one's coping style. Beliefs can either soften the impact of a stressor or distort its proportions.

Resources constitute another mediating factor in the adaptation to stressful life-events such as an impairment. Resources can be divided into personal ones, such as 'positive appraisal' (denial, wishful thinking) and 'reframing' (redefining a problem so that it appears less stressful), and socio-ecological ones, such as social or spiritual support, financial and/or professional help. Beliefs affect resources, which in turn affect coping behaviour, eventually reconstructing both beliefs and resources in a circular way. For example, professionals can be perceived as offering valuable advice, constituting a useful resource, or alternatively, as interfering and confusing, adding to the stress rather than reducing it. Similarly, the extended family can be perceived as offering childcare, and therefore as a valuable resource, or alternatively, as unable to understand and cope with the impairment.

Change will be greatly facilitated if the therapist is seen as understanding and appreciating the family's particular coping style, and if he or she reinforces whatever coping strategies are helpful to the family. Sometimes, this is all the 'treatment' that is needed.

However, if it becomes evident during the assessment process that some of the family's or the hearing-impaired individual's perceptions are distorted in so far as they prevent adaptation and growth – for example, by limiting use of resources – then cognitive therapy would seem the treatment of choice. In cognitive therapy, the therapist adopts a Socratic style of questioning to help the client identify, analyse and challenge thoughts, beliefs and assumptions about him or herself and the world. Practical exercises might be set up to help gather 'evidence' for and against the beliefs held.

If the assessment process reveals that the family perceives existing external resources to be insufficient, then practical aid should be provided, such as increased professional input in the form of teaching, speech therapy and/or better amplification, or anything else the family see as missing. Alternatively, internal resources such as parenting skills might be lacking, and behaviour therapy aimed at increasing the parents' ability to set and implement boundaries and to manage temper tantrums, bedwetting or sleep problems could be provided.

However, sometimes it might transpire during the assessment process that parents possess the necessary parenting skills, but are unable to use these because they have not as yet accepted the impairment. In this case, counselling should be provided for the parents to help them explore the feelings surrounding the impairment.

Similarly, hearing-impaired teenagers who grieve because they may have experienced rejection by the opposite sex, or begin to fully realise the permanency of their hearing loss, may express this grief in reduced school attendance or poor school performance, despite adequate abilities. Counselling would in all probability be more effective than increased teaching input.

In some families, dysfunctional patterns of interaction between family members existed long before the diagnosis of the hearing impairment was made, which then serves to amplify the existing difficulties. For example, a hearing-impaired child may present with a number of behavioural problems which have the function of re-uniting the parents by focusing on the 'problem child'. This may be a coping strategy for the parents, but at a considerable cost to the child. Therapeutic interventions will have to be directed at the family as a whole, focusing on the family members' pattern of interaction rather than on the so-called 'problem child'.

References

Bax, M., Hart, H. and Jenkins, S. (1983) 'The Behaviour, Development and Health of the Young Child: Implications for Care', *British Medical Journal*, Vol. 286, pp.1, 793–6.

Beresford, B. (1994) 'Resources and Strategies: How Parents Cope with the Care of a Disabled Child', *Journal of Child Psychology and Psychiatry*, Vol. 35, No. 1, pp.171–209.

Carter, B. and McGoldrick, M. (eds) (1989) *The Changing Family Life Cycle: A Framework for Family Therapy* (2nd edn), New York: Allyn and Bacon.

Gaudet, L. and Powers, G.M. (1989) 'Systems Treatment in Paediatric Chronic Illness: A Parent Group Programme', *Family Systems Medicine*, Vol. 7, No. 1, pp.90–9.

Hindley, P.A., Hill, P.D., McGuigan, S. and Kitson, S. (1994) 'Psychiatric Disorder in Deaf and Hearing Impaired Children and Young People: A Prevalence Study', *Journal of Child Psychology and Psychiatry*, Vol. 35, No. 5, pp.917–34.

Kaplan, G.J., Fleshman, J.K., Bonder, T.R., Baum, C. and Clark, P.S. (1973) 'Long Term Effects of Otitis Media: A Ten-year Cohort Study of Alaskan Eskimo Children', *Pediatrics*, Vol. 52, pp.577–85.

Lazarus, R.S. and Folkman, S. (1984) 'Coping and Adaptation', in Gentry, W.D. (ed.) *Handbook of Behavioural Medicine*, New York: Guildford Press.

Patterson, J. and McCubbin, H. (1983) 'Chronic Illness: Family Stress and Coping', in Figley, C. and McCubbin, H. (eds) *Stress and the Family*, New York: Brunner/Mazel.

Rapin, E. (1979) 'Conductive Hearing Loss: Effect on Children's Language Scholastic Skills – A Review of the Literature', *Annals of Otology, Rhinology and Laryngology*, Vol. 89, pp.303–11.
Sak, R. and Ruben, R.J. (1981) 'Recurrent Middle Ear Effusion in Childhood: Implications of Temporary Auditory Deprivation for Language Learning', *Annals of Otology, Rhinology and Laryngology*, Vol. 89, pp.303–11.

Further reading

Brown, D. and Peddar, J. (1980) *Introduction to Psychotherapy – An Outline of Psychodynamic Principles and Practice*, London and New York: Tavistock Publications.
Cottrell, D. and Summers, R. (1989) 'Communicating an Evolutionary Diagnosis of Disability to Parents', *Child Care, Health and Development*, No. 16, pp.211–18.
Elliott, C.D., Murray, D.J. and Pearson, L.S. (1983) *British Ability Scales*, London: Nfer-Nelson.
Harvey, M. (1989) *Psychotherapy with Deaf and Hard of Hearing Persons: A Systematic Model*, Hillsdale, New Jersey: Lawrence Erlbaum Associates.
Hawton, K., Salkovskis, P.M., Kirk, J. and Clark, D.M. (1989) *Cognitive Behaviour Therapy for Psychiatric Problems: A Practical Guide*, Oxford, New York and Tokyo: Oxford Medical Publications.
Hiskey, M.S. (1955) *Hiskey-Nebraska Test of Learning Aptitude*, Lincoln, Nebraska: College View Printers.
Neale, M.D. (1989) *Neale Analysis of Reading Ability – Revised British Edition*, London: Nfer-Nelson.
Paget, S. (1983) 'Long-term Grieving in Parents of Hearing-impaired Children: A Synthesis of Parental Experience', *Journal of the British Association of the Deaf*, Vol. 7, No. 3, pp.78–82.
Schonell, F.J. and Schonell, F.E. (1950) *Schonell Graded Word Spelling Test*, London: Oliver and Boyd.
Snijders, J.T. and Snijders-Oomen, N. (1976) *Snijders-Oomen Non-verbal Intelligence Scale S.O.N. 2 1/2–7*, Haarlem: H.D. Tjeenk, Willink Groninger.
Webster, A. (1986) *Deafness, Development and Literacy*, London and New York: Methuen.
Wechsler, D. (1990) *Wechsler Preschool and Primary Scale of Intelligence – Revised*, Sidcup, Kent: Psychological Corporation/Harcourt, Brace Jovanovich.
Wechsler, D. (1992) *Wechsler Intelligence Scale for Children – Third Edition UK*, Sidcup, Kent: Psychological Corporation/Harcourt, Brace Jovanovich.
Worden, W.F. (1983) *Grief Counselling and Grief Therapy*, London: Routledge.

4 Physical disabilities

Frank Steel

Introduction

In 1966 a collection of essays was published under the generic title *Stigma: The Experience of Disability* (Hunt, 1966). The contributors provided a special insight into what disability meant to them; and, given that they were all physically disabled, their experiences made them particularly qualified to share their personal views on the impact of disability, and to write from a uniquely authoritative standpoint. One of the contributors, Louis Battye, wrote with a directness which he readily admitted might cause offence, and yet his message is all the more powerful because it dares to confront some of the central issues relating to disability:

> The cripple is an object of Christian charity, a socio-medical problem, a stumbling nuisance, and an embarrassment to the girl he falls in love with. He is a vocation for saints, a livelihood for the manufacturers of wheelchairs, a target for busybodies, and a means by which prosperous citizens assuage their consciences. He is at the mercy of over-worked doctors and nurses and under-worked bureaucrats and social investigators. He is pitied and ignored, helped and patronised, understood and stared at. But he is hardly ever taken seriously as a *man*. (Battye, 1966, p.15)

Battye was writing as a mature, articulate adult, and the bitter experiences he had encountered as a consequence of his disability are patently clear. A child with a physical disability, however, is unlikely to be in a position of being able to fully identify the source of his or her frustrations and fears, much less comprehend them, and will be exposed to experiences which are often uncomfortable – on a social, emotional or physical level – and frequently stress-inducing.

To understand the nature of physical disability, even to a small degree, is to appreciate how complex an area it is, and how easy it is to make rash generalisations and naive assumptions. As soon as a child or adult is labelled as being 'disabled' or 'handicapped', barriers are erected, either consciously or unconsciously. The words are value-laden, charged with unfortunate and often misleading connotations. The medical model of disability – which focused almost exclusively on the physical causation of impairment and its treatment, and viewed the disabled person more as a patient than as an individual with a range of needs – was replaced by the concept of 'special educational needs' (SEN) in the Warnock Report (DES, 1978) and enshrined within the Education Act 1981. However, the medical perspective still lingers, and still presents a potential stumbling-block which can influence the way in which a child is perceived, and, by inference, the manner in which the child perceives him or herself. All of us experience a measure of frustration or failure or rejection at different times; indeed, it is part of the human psyche. How we cope is determined by the amount of support which we receive, the coping strategies which we have developed to combat life's setbacks, and the inner resources which we can draw upon. If our experience has been one of rejection, of personal adversity, of constant frustration or disappointment, of limitations imposed upon us, then our self-esteem is likely to be impaired and our coping mechanisms underdeveloped. If, in addition, the views of the people we encounter are coloured by suspicion, guilt, ignorance or uncertainty, our perception of the world is likely to be somewhat distorted, and the existence of stress in our lives a constant reminder that we are not wholly 'normal', not fully accepted by society, and almost certainly not a full participant within it.

By its very nature, physical disability can be alarming, both to the person who experiences it as an intrinsic part of their existence as well as to the person who encounters it from an external perspective. It can present a very real barrier which may compromise meaningful communication and social interaction. Its existence can mask the individual who has to live behind the veil of disability. Little wonder, then, that children with a physical disability are prey to any number of stressful situations in their lives.

However, the degree to which they might suffer from stress is not intrinsically linked to any particular disability, nor necessarily associated with any specific combination of circumstances. Children with minimal disabilities might experience acute embarrassment as a consequence of their own perceptions of their appearance, their gait or their physical limitations, while those with more profound and significant handicaps might be totally oblivious to the social nuances of their situation. There are no hard and fast rules. To an extent, working closely with children with physical disabilities is working in uncharted territory: each child has his or her own experiences and expectations, and his or her own strategies for dealing with the problems which he or she faces.

Stresses related to physical disability

'Physical disability' is the term applied to a wide range of medical conditions which can result in temporary or permanent impairment. If the degree of impairment is such that it radically impedes or precludes normal physical or cognitive functioning, then it constitutes a 'handicap'. The implications of a particular disability may vary significantly, so that its effect has to be gauged across a broad continuum. 'Cerebral palsy', for example, is an umbrella term which describes an abnormality of physical functioning which can be severe or mild. Children with cerebral palsy may be totally dependent, doubly incontinent, have a range of sensory impairments, be unable to communicate, and have severe learning difficulties. Equally, they might exhibit minor physical difficulties in terms of mobility, experience some problem with fine motor co-ordination, and yet function perfectly adequately both socially and academically. The parameters of disability are inevitably broad, and the implications of any one disability cannot automatically be generalised to others. As with any individual, circumstances vary according to a number of factors, and one person's response to their disability may not necessarily mirror that of another. So, too, with their response to stress.

For children with physical disabilities, stress may manifest itself, first and foremost, as a reaction to their condition and the restrictions and constraints which it imposes on them. The most obvious difficulties are those which are present by virtue of the degree of physical impairment. The inability to perform even the most simple of physical tasks is something which is associated with a range of physical disabilities.

Example: Karen

Karen is 5 years old and has spastic quadriplegia, a severe form of cerebral palsy which affects all four limbs and inhibits fine and gross movements. Such is the extent of her impairment, it is unlikely that she will ever be able to walk. Although she is unable to speak, Karen communicates by means of gesture and facial expressions, and is very responsive to adults. The observations of her parents, health visitors, therapists and the education staff who have worked with her suggest that she is functioning cognitively within the moderate range of learning difficulty.

Karen's ability to control her movements is extremely limited, and she has difficulty maintaining her posture. In infancy, she was unable to achieve sitting balance and head control and had little command over the most basic of hand and arm movements. Motivation can be affected if the child's efforts to control movements and influence the environment are constantly frustrated, and the effects of such potentially stressful situations have to be countered. Karen experienced many such early difficulties and responded tearfully, often exhibiting temper tantrums and occasionally displaying signs of apathy or withdrawal.

Helping Karen to gain some degree of mastery over her world and achieve a measure of independence was an important aim in these early years, and the stresses related to her inability to exercise autonomy and control were gradually reduced, with small, incremental successes leading to significant achievement. Karen's parents, supported by the physiotherapist and occupational therapist, were encouraged to undertake a programme of exercises and directed movements aimed at promoting co-ordination and strengthening muscle tone. These were aided by the provision of specially adapted equipment for seating, which allowed Karen to be comfortably positioned so that her energy could be utilised more effectively. Such programmes were often intensive, and required perseverance and determination on the part of both Karen and her parents. After several years following these programmes, Karen is now able to sit unsupported, can use directed movements to operate a switch which allows access to appropriate software on her computer, and this, in turn, has provided her with a more sophisticated form of communication. The earlier stress-inducing frustrations have largely been overcome now that Karen can interact in a more meaningful way with her environment, and the episodes of withdrawal and outbursts of temper have been all but eradicated.

Whilst the more profound effects of cerebral palsy result in this degree of acute handicap, it can also occur in some of the degenerative and debilitating conditions, such as muscular dystrophy. The inability to control one's own body, being denied the opportunity of exploring one's immediate environment or taking pleasure in the exercise of control over simple events and functions (as in the case of Karen) is a fundamental loss of the most basic kind. It poses a virtually unassailable barrier for the child, particularly in the early years of development, and prevents him or her experiencing many of the ordinary pleasures and achievements of childhood. It renders the child vulnerable to external forces and entirely dependent on adult intervention.

Dependence as a source of stress

Dependence on others, particularly when related to the most basic and intimate of functions, is a potential source of stress. If a child is both dependent and incontinent, the routines associated with bathroom management have to be carefully and sensitively handled if a stress-free situation is to be created. Imagine, in the first instance, the frustration which a child (and particularly an adolescent) must feel at not being able to perform his or her own care routines. It is by no means uncommon for adolescent boys to be changed by female carers; and, at a time when their able-bodied peers are undergoing the emotional and sexual changes associated with puberty and adolescence and enjoying greater freedom and independence, the smallest indignity can produce feelings of anxiety, inadequacy and resentment.

Carers must be particularly sensitive to the feelings of the child for whom they are performing the most intimate of care routines, and be alert to the potential irritations and oversights which may produce stress, apprehension or impatience in the child. A fixed routine, where the child is taken to the bathroom at a set time and expected to perform on cue, can produce acute embarrassment and a level of stress which would be deemed unacceptable in any other individual. This restriction of choice may extend to include the personal hygiene items which are used. Teenage girls, for example, are usually at liberty to choose the type of sanitary towels which they prefer, and certainly wish to cope with their monthly cycle as discreetly as possible. Unfortunately, it is not unknown for carers to inadvertently broadcast the fact that 'she's got her period', and such instances, apart from demonstrating a distinct lack of empathy, are inexcusable. A lack of privacy within the bathroom management areas, with curtaining the only form of screening, can also add to the indignity of the situation.

Experienced carers have a repertoire of skills which they employ to ensure that the dignity and comfort of the child are preserved at all times. They appreciate that the child in their care is an individual, with feelings which can easily be hurt. They are careful not to make insensitive remarks in front of the child, and refrain from discussing him or her as though referring to an invisible participant. They will listen to the child and respond sensitively to any anxieties which he or she might have. Above all, they will appreciate that the child is not an item on a conveyor belt – someone to be processed through the bathroom as quickly as possible. They will exercise patience and tact, and understand that, for a child who is constrained within a wheelchair for much of the time, the least discomfort can be a major distraction. Clothing will be adjusted accordingly, and the physical handling of the child performed with confidence and an appropriate degree of care. They will intuitively know that having to ask for assistance may be perplexing for the child, and will attempt to interpret his or her needs with the minimum of fuss. And they will understand that any minor irritation which they may inadvertently show, any exasperation which they might express through careless remarks or their body language and manner, will be transmitted to the child and may elicit a stressful response. With sensitivity and empathy, such traumas can be avoided, and the self-esteem and dignity of the child maintained.

Dependency brings with it other potential problems. The dependency of a child on an unfamiliar adult may evoke feelings of disquiet and helplessness, particularly in the area of physical management and handling. For instance, an inexperienced carer might lack the knowledge or confidence to position a child correctly, or be unable to perform transferences from one surface to another using the recommended method. Any lack of confidence which the child might have in his or her carer will be translated into stress, and induce high levels of anxiety.

Example: Robert

Robert, a teenager with brittle bones (osteogenesis imperfecta), experienced acute dread whenever he needed to be transferred from his wheelchair. Extreme care had to be exercised during such a manoeuvre, since the least pressure could result in a fracture, and Robert had sustained many such fractures throughout childhood. As a result, his whole life was underscored by a degree of insecurity and anxiety associated with his condition, and the daily risk of being subjected to yet more damage as a result of his vulnerability.

Robert's problem is obviously something of an extreme, and yet poor handling and physical management strategies which are undertaken without due care and consideration can elicit a similar degree of trepidation in children who are physically dependent. In Robert's case, a long-term strategy designed to reduce his stressful reaction to his physical management was devised in conjunction with Robert and his carers, whereby he was encouraged to exercise full control and take charge of the situation. This entailed providing Robert with every opportunity to advise and direct his helpers, instruct them as to when he was ready for a particular manoeuvre, and thus ensure that transfers were effected smoothly and with appropriate care. Such tasks were never rushed, and never undertaken until Robert was fully prepared. This strategy subsequently generated a strong bond of trust between Robert and his carers, and helped to eliminate much of the stress he had previously experienced.

Communication difficulties

Communication disorders in children with physical disabilities are invariably another potential cause of stress. The ability to communicate effectively, to be allowed to make choices, to interact with parents, friends, carers and the wider community, are all essential in the development and well-being of the individual. Any disruption to this process is likely to generate degrees of stress and frustration which, to an extent, will be contingent on the factors which apply to the specific individual. A child with profound and multiple learning difficulties (PMLD) may be unable to communicate for a variety of reasons, all of which may compound the process. The level of language acquisition may be severely impaired as a result of severe learning difficulties; social awareness may be further restricted because of visual and/or auditory impairment, and articulation may be restricted to the most basic verbal utterances due to muscular impairment and a lack of control over the organs which govern the production of sounds and speech.

For the pupil with PMLD who has a basic awareness of his or her environment, and the desire to communicate, the problems experienced because of difficulty in making his or her needs apparent will provoke a measure of anxiety, especially if that need is for a drink, or the need to be repositioned because of discomfort, or the necessity to use the toilet. Teachers and carers need to be particularly receptive to the forms of non-verbal communication which the child may use; these will include eye-pointing, gesture, facial expressions and a number of other subtle interactions which, through close observation, can be interpreted and acted upon. For children with the ability to utilise more sophisticated forms of communication, a range of additional and alternative aids are available. Some children will be able to use a system utilising symbols, such as Blissymbolics charts or Makaton symbols; others may be able to communicate through the use of gesture and signing, with signs such as those used in Makaton supplemented by the appropriate symbol.

Additional forms of communication necessitate the use of special communication aids. A Lightwriter, for example, allows the child to use a small, conventional keyboard to type out a message, whilst communication systems which permit short messages to be recorded and played back at the touch of a button include devices such as the Orac. For children whose main difficulty is that of articulation, such devices can be extremely effective in allowing them to communicate their essential needs, and enable them to participate more fully in group activities.

Teaching a child to use an appropriate communication aid requires an investment of time and patience; similarly, permitting him or her to have access to the particular aid when required, and giving him or her the opportunity to use it, necessitates both sensitivity and patience. How annoying it must be for the child when the listener does not allow the time or chance to respond, or does not provide sufficient opportunity to express a particular preference. It is largely due to the social ineptness of others, particularly adults, that such occasions can provide a constant source of stress and indignation for the child with communication difficulties. A lack of sensitivity or awareness on the part of the adult, resulting in the child being overlooked or ignored, allied to impatience or an attitude of curt dismissal, may result in the child feeling frustrated, anxious, patronised, inadequate and undervalued. All of these may contribute to a debilitating and confidence-sapping feeling of stress, which will adversely affect the child's performance socially, emotionally and, most likely, academically.

Gaining access to the curriculum

Poor academic performance can be an acute cause of distress in children with physical disabilities, particularly if learning difficulties are an associated feature of their condition. Difficulties in reading, writing and communication may produce negative and disquieting feelings of inadequacy in pupils who experience failure with depressing regularity. Combating this and providing pupils with the opportunity to experience success is a major aim for the school, be it special or mainstream. Access to the curriculum is an obvious prerequisite. At the level of physical access, for those pupils whose fine motor skills do not provide them with the ability to write, paint, draw or manipulate objects in any practical sense, information technology (IT) has provided a gateway to the curriculum. In the non-statutory guidance for IT which was produced by the National Curriculum Council in 1990, the importance of IT for pupils with special educational needs was underlined:

> All pupils have an entitlement to develop IT capability. Pupils who are unable to communicate conventionally because of physical or sensory impairment, may have access to the curriculum only through information technology. (NCC, 1990, para. 4.1)

Since computer technology was first introduced into schools as a means of ensuring that pupils with special needs were enabled to participate fully in the curriculum, a range of specialised software, access devices and learning aids has been produced. As Roberts (1991) observes:

> Concept keyboard based wordprocessors put reporting and creative writing within the grasp of some pupils who lack the otherwise necessary handwriting skills. Switches can open up new horizons for many pupils with profound and multiple learning difficulties in controlling and exploring their environment. (p.176)

Access to the curriculum via the physical medium of IT is not the only form of access which has to be facilitated. For pupils with learning difficulties – and many pupils with a physical disability have mild, moderate or severe learning difficulties as a result of injury to the brain – a carefully structured curriculum is essential if progress is to be made and achievement ensured. The range of problems which a child with a physical disability may have to cope with can be legion. Poor short-term memory, difficulties in sequencing, poor concentration and motivation, being easily distracted and an inability to generalise knowledge or transfer skills from one setting to another are some of the main problems which may interfere with the learning process. Some or all of these may be exhibited by pupils in mainstream education, and strategies have to be implemented in order to prevent boredom, negativity and stress from adversely influencing their performance.

Special schools have developed a variety of approaches and methods which might usefully be employed within the mainstream setting to support the learning potential of pupils with special needs. For those pupils with severe learning difficulties who are educated within a special school, highly structured curricula have been devised which reduce major learning goals to a series of manageable steps through which the child may progress at his or her own pace. The aim of a 'developmental curriculum' has been described by the DES and Welsh Office as 'covering selected and sharply focused educational, social and other experiences with precisely defined objectives and designed to encourage a measure of personal autonomy' (DES/WO, 1984, p.2).

A similar approach to curriculum design and delivery has long been advocated by other practitioners in the field: Coupe and Porter (1986), Carpenter (1987), Ouvry (1987) and Longhorn (1991) are just a few of those who have devised special curricula for pupils with severe learning difficulties and developed approaches for use with children with PMLD.

Other approaches have been produced for use with children with moderate learning difficulties, with behavioural objectives providing a framework for carefully structured intervention programmes and prescriptive teaching techniques. Ainscow and Tweddle (1979) have long been advocates of this particular approach, and have written and lectured extensively on the need to set precise behavioural objectives, to use task analysis techniques, and the importance of implementing systematic, classroom-based assessment as a means of preventing failure for pupils with special educational needs (SEN). As a method of ensuring success and focusing on achievement – and thereby mediating the effects of stress engendered as a result of the experience of classroom failure – these approaches should not be discounted, or their impact undervalued.

The introduction of the National Curriculum has provided the impetus for many schools to review their curriculum and ensure that all their pupils have access to a broad, balanced and relevant curriculum. The need to ensure continuity and progression and provide for differentiation within the curriculum has resulted in detailed planning and the publication of a range of books which have inspired classroom practitioners to seek new approaches and ensure that their SEN pupils can reap the benefit of carefully structured and engaging lessons. For children with physical disabilities, the need to achieve a measure of success and participate fully in a range of activities is essential, especially since their particular disabilities may exclude them from other experiences and opportunities.

Adolescence and the stress of rejection

For some children with physical disabilities, the gradual feelings of rejection which they experience during their formative years can be extremely stressful, and all the more acute since they cannot fully comprehend why this should be so. A child of nursery age will often be pampered by adults and enjoy being the centre of attention. As young, often attractive, vulnerable children, they strike a maternal/paternal chord in many adults, and their age often masks the more significant aspects of their disability. A child in an ordinary pushchair will elicit little comment when of nursery age; thereafter, confinement to a wheelchair will most certainly be noticed. Similarly, a non-communicating child may survive with a limited repertoire of facial expressions and smiles while in infancy, but will find it increasingly difficult to engage the attention of an adult without the use of speech. As the child matures, the limitations imposed by the disability may become more pronounced. If a child experiences difficulties in mobility, his or her gait may become increasingly awkward and emphasise the fact that he or she is disabled.

The onset of puberty, with all the side-effects which bedevil even able-bodied adolescents, may further serve to make the physically disabled teenager feel less attractive, especially if his or her personal hygiene is difficult to maintain without adult supervision. The normal feelings of confusion, identity crisis and anxiety engendered by adolescence may be further exacerbated by the feelings of isolation and rejection experienced as a consequence of the disability. Such feelings might have crystallised over a number of years. As the children's appearance changes; as they, perhaps, become increasingly ungainly in their movements; as they become more dependent; as access to clubs and activities is increasingly restricted; as the gap between normal physical development and normal social interactions widens – all of these factors may precipitate feelings of depression, increasing isolation and frustration, and impair psychological adjustment to a significant degree. Counselling might be required at this stage if the adolescent is to be supported and encouraged through this potentially traumatic period of adjustment.

The stress of family relationships

Tensions within the family may produce a major source of stress for the child. The parents of a disabled child are often in need of support if they are to adjust to the realities of the situation. Furneaux (1988) lists some of the main factors which the parents and families of a handicapped child will need to address if they are to cope with their responsibilities and, in turn, provide support for their child. They require reassurance, practical assistance, relevant information and someone in whom they can confide; they also need to feel that they are still individuals in their own right, not just the parents of a handicapped child. They will also need time to spend with their partners, and an opportunity to have some time away from the demands of parenting. Perhaps, above all, they will need to be shown how they can take the initiative and help to provide effective support for their child.

If the needs of the parents are neglected, it is a distinct possibility that stress will be one of the results, and such stress will invariably be transmitted to the child. There are many examples of parents communicating tensions to their children. Unfavourable comparisons with an able-bodied sibling might easily produce feelings of inadequacy and guilt, and reinforce low self-esteem. Parental expectations may be unrealistically high, without reference to the realities and limitations of their child's disability. This might be linked to academic expectations or, in the case of a child with cerebral palsy, high expectations that they will achieve full mobility and independence. Parents often pin their hopes on new approaches and forms of treatment, thinking they might be a panacea which will effect a 'cure' for their child.

Conductive Education has inspired many parents with such hopes for their child. Sometimes, however, these hopes cannot be realised. Children may not respond favourably to the demands of such an intensive regime, and parents may be overly zealous in their desire to achieve quantifiable success for their non-ambulant child. The demands required of both parent and child may eventually prove to be overwhelming, with family routines disrupted, siblings feeling that their needs are being ignored because of the amount of attention invested in their disabled brother or sister, and tensions being generated as efforts may fail to achieve the desired outcomes. If the expectations which the parents have are constantly dashed, increased consternation often results. These frustrations, tensions and feelings of guilt may be unconsciously projected onto the child, and a downward spiral of negative feedback and poor self-esteem may be generated.

It is not uncommon for family tensions to be created as a result of the parents pursuing recompense from the health authority for damage caused to their child. If they are involved in litigation and seeking damages, conflicts may arise which place the child under additional stress. Such cases are invariably protracted, often spanning a number of years, and the resulting stress may subsequently induce long-term psychological damage for the child and other members of the family. During this time, the child may be required to undertake various assessments and reviews. Such an emphasis on his or her disability may prove distressing, particularly if the child perceives that it is a cause of conflict between his or her parents. If, as is sometimes the case, the parents become involved in a 'crusade' against what they may see as a bureaucratic and uncaring system, it is often at the expense of the family unit. Stress may be unconsciously transferred to the child, who may neither have the resources to cope with such complex emotions and reactions nor the ability to comprehend them.

The provision of support for the parents of disabled children from the moment of diagnosis, through the early years, and into adulthood can be a major factor in reducing stress within the family and, by implication, removing some of the uncertainties and perceptions which can adversely affect the child. Community health services, family support groups, parent groups and district disability teams can all offer different services and support mechanisms to the family. Portage schemes, with their emphasis on practical, home-based intervention programmes, can encourage the parents of a disabled child to participate in his or her early development, and can create a foundation for future interaction with other professionals. Offering practical support through respite care schemes can allow the family to enjoy short, regular breaks, as can holiday schemes and home-based intervention schemes. Opportunities can then develop which will allow parents to share their problems and seek assistance, as required, on their terms. As reported by Lacey and Lomas (1993): 'A specialist social worker once stated that he saw his main aim when working with parents as developing their communication skills in order to help them express their needs, hopes, fears and desires for their child' (p.155).

Once a child with special needs has been placed within school, a network of support can be made available to the parents. This support is particularly evident within the context of a special school. Access to a physiotherapist, occupational therapist and speech therapist can encourage the parents to reinforce therapy programmes at home, and may help them to accept a realistic view of their child's potential, while at the same time inspiring them to work positively with whatever strengths their child possesses. Additional guidance and advice can be obtained from an educational psychologist, and medical problems and concerns can be discussed with the senior clinical medical officer or paediatrician who has medical oversight of the child. As the child prepares for the transition from school to an appropriate post-school placement, the support of a specialist careers officer will be provided, and a disablement assessment officer may be involved in order to identify the particular requirements stemming from the child's special educational needs. In addition to providing support for the child's family through advice, guidance, practical workshops and, when appropriate, counselling, the various professionals will also work directly with the child.

The most distressing aspects of disability are ultimately those relating to the child with a terminal condition. No amount of support or counselling can totally prepare a family for the loss of a child, or cushion them against the effects of bereavement which they will experience. Degenerative conditions such as muscular dystrophy and acute long-term illnesses tax the patience and fortitude of the most resilient of parents, since any hope of their child recovering is denied them. For children with a degenerative condition, the effects of a steady decline from normality to a state of total dependence and increasing ill health can be devastating. They may lose touch with their able-bodied friends and become increasingly isolated. They will be able to remember the activities in which they could participate, and mourn the loss of their independence. If they transfer from a mainstream school to a special school, as many of them do once the condition has resulted in irreversible deterioration, they may make friends with others who have a similar disability and an equally poor prognosis. Some of their friends may die. They will have to cope with this grief, as well as with the effects of their own disability, aware that, for them, time is limited.

Strategies to counter stress

How, as professionals and carers, can we help to support pupils with physical disabilities and either reduce or help them to cope with the numerous stresses with which they may be confronted? Understanding and empathy, allied to the skills necessary to provide a secure and supportive environment, are an obvious starting point. As Gulliford and Upton (1992) advocate, a special knowledge and understanding of the 'impairments and disabilities which may contribute to the development of handicap and may limit educational progress' (p.1) will offer a specific basis for effective support and intervention. The Warnock Report (DES, 1978) recognised the importance of training for the teachers of pupils with SEN, stating that: 'In-service training will be vital if teachers are to help effectively in recognising the children who have special educational needs and in making suitable provision for them' (para. 12.4).

There are a number of practical strategies which can be adopted in attempting to deal effectively with children in stress and provide them with the support which they require:

- Identify situations which create stress, and endeavour to minimise or eradicate them.
- Learn to recognise signs of stress in particular children, and develop appropriate intervention strategies.
- Provide a consistent and secure environment.
- Exercise patience and sensitivity.
- Adopt a calm and empathetic approach.
- Be prepared to listen and respond to a child's anxieties.

- Recognise success and achievement, no matter how small, and promote self-esteem and feelings of worth.
- Learn some of the essential skills of counselling.
- Use humour to defuse confrontational or anxiety-inducing situations.
- Set realistic and achievable goals for the child.
- Modify tasks and provide alternatives; make them accessible.
- Avoid off-loading personal tensions and frustrations on the child.
- Allow the child to exercise choice, explore independence and experience a feeling of control.
- Respect the child's rights as an individual, and preserve his or her dignity and self-esteem.
- Develop competencies in physical management tasks in order to inspire confidence in the child.
- Attend awareness training seminars on the implications of disability, to increase your knowledge and understanding.
- Be prepared to share information with colleagues on what was successful, and be prepared to learn from them.
- Recognise that there are often no short-term solutions in dealing with stress.

Conclusion

Any detailed or exhaustive coverage of stress in children with physical disabilities is not possible in a single chapter of a book. Issues such as the stress induced by the key transition periods of entry into school, transfer to secondary education and the anxieties created by uncertain career prospects or enforced leisure have not been explored. Neither have I attempted to include the problems associated with disability in the adolescent years, which would include the inevitable themes of sexuality, the restrictions imposed by overprotective parents and the environmental and social obstacles presented by society's general ineptness in coping with disabled individuals.

As Pugh and De'Ath (1989) point out: 'No two parents, no two children, are the same nor will they have the same needs, nor will those needs remain constant over a period of time' (p.62). We can offer guidance and support, empathy and understanding, and try to generalise our experience so that it may be of some practical use. Ultimately, however, the children or young people will have to deal with stress and anxiety and personal setbacks, each in their own way. We cannot always be there to fight their battles for them. What we can do, nevertheless, as parents, carers, educators or therapists, is to take on the roles of advocate, mediator and facilitator. We can attempt to equip them with the strategies to cope; provide support and encouragement along the way; set realistic goals and aspirations; exercise patience and tact; be sensitive to their needs and aware of our own limitations and short-comings; moderate our demands; increase our skills, and create a caring environment in which the child might learn to feel valued.

References

Ainscow, M. and Tweddle, D. (1979) *Preventing Classroom Failure: An Objectives Approach*, Chichester: John Wiley.
Battye, L. (1966) 'The Chatterley Syndrome', in Hunt, P. (ed.) *Stigma: The Experience of Disability*, London: Geoffrey Chapman.
Carpenter, B. (1987) 'Curriculum planning for children with profound and multiple learning difficulties', *Early Child Development and Care*, Vol. 28, No. 2, pp.149–62.
Coupe, J. and Porter, J. (eds) (1986) *The Education of Children with Severe Learning Difficulties*, London: Croom Helm.
DES (Department of Education and Science) (1978) *Special Educational Needs: Report of the Committee of Inquiry into the Education of Handicapped Children and Young People*, London: HMSO (The Warnock Report).
DES/WO (Department of Education and Science/Welsh Office) (1984) *The Organisation and Content of the Curriculum: Special Schools*, London: HMSO.
Furneaux, B. (1988) *Special Parents*, Milton Keynes: Open University Press.
Gulliford, R. and Upton, G. (eds) (1992) *Special Educational Needs*, London: Routledge.
Hunt, P. (ed.) (1966) *Stigma: The Experience of Disability*, London: Geoffrey Chapman.
Lacey, P. and Lomas, J. (1993) *Support Services and the Curriculum: A Practical Guide to Collaboration*, London: David Fulton.
Longhorn, F. (1991) 'A Sensory Science Curriculum', in Ashdown, R., Carpenter, B. and Bovair, K. (eds) *The Curriculum Challenge*, London: Falmer Press.
NCC (National Curriculum Council) (1990) *Technology: Non-statutory Guidance for Information Technology*, York: National Curriculum Council.
Ouvry, C. (1987) *Educating Children with Profound Handicaps*, Kidderminster: British Institute for Mental Handicap.
Pugh, G. and De'Ath, E. (eds) (1989) *Working towards Partnership in the Early Years*, London: National Children's Bureau.
Roberts, P. (1991) 'Cross-curricular Approaches to Information Technology', in Ashdown, R., Carpenter, B. and Bovair, K. (eds) *The Curriculum Challenge*, London: Falmer Press.

Further reading

Anderson, E.M. and Clarke, L. (1982) *Disability in Adolescence*, London: Methuen.
Ashdown, R., Carpenter, B. and Bovair, K. (eds) (1991) *The Curriculum Challenge*, London: Falmer Press.
Boswell, D.M. and Wingrove, J.M. (eds) (1974) *The Handicapped Person in the Community*, London: Open University/Tavistock Publications.

DES/WO (Department of Education and Science/Welsh Office) (1989) *English in the National Curriculum*, London: HMSO.

DES/WO (Department of Education and Science/Welsh Office) (1990) *Technology in the National Curriculum*, London: HMSO.

Longhorn, F. (1988) *A Sensory Curriculum for Very Special People: A Practical Approach to Curriculum Planning*, Human Horizons Series, London: Souvenir Press.

Male, J. and Thompson, C. (1985) *The Educational Implications of Disability*, London: Royal Association for Disability and Rehabilitation.

Tilstone, C. (ed.) (1991) *Teaching Pupils with Severe Learning Difficulties: Practical Approaches*, London: David Fulton.

5   Gifted children

Joan Freeman

Introduction

It is impossible to be sure who the 'gifted' are: there are dozens of definitions, most of which refer to children's advancement on psychological tests measuring different kinds of achievements. These may be high marks in school subjects or high scores on tests of ability. But non-school subjects, such as social talents or potential business acumen, are rarely considered. Although conventional intelligence tests resulting in an IQ score are often used for identification, they are not an entirely sensitive measure of very high intellect, because of the 'ceiling effect', the upper limit of the tests being too low to distinguish between the top few per cent. IQ scores are often misunderstood and misused – for example, they are not designed to identify personal styles of thinking, personality or life-skills; in fact, they are very poor at predicting success in the world outside the school gates (Subotnik et al., 1993, p.115).

Yet, however it is defined and measured, intelligence is universally recognised as taking some part in the complex dynamics of exceptionally high-level performance in most areas of endeavour, along with personality and opportunity. But when intelligence and personality types were compared in 500 12-year-olds, although both characteristics were found to be linked with attitudes to schoolwork, each was independent of the other – ability could not predict personality and vice versa (Marjoriebanks, 1992). However, this confusion about the definition and measurement of giftedness does not affect the common assumption that gifted children – who are, in that sense, abnormal – must suffer some stress because they live among people who are almost always less able than they are.

Stress and abilities

Stress is brought about by a situation which demands adjustment from an individual and which results in a stress reaction, involving both physiological and psycho-social aspects. Physiologically, at the extremes, the acute stress of shock produces a surge of adrenalin, whereas long-term adaptation to stress produces a higher metabolic rate and blood glucose level, which can lower levels of energy and suppress the body's immune system (Kennedy et al., 1990). Psychologically, we respond not only to present threats, but also to symbols of stressors and expectations of them, which can produce depression, anxiety, and underachievement. Children (like the elderly) are often the most susceptible to stress, especially at critical periods of their development, because they have fewer coping resources to deal with it.

Stress is unlikely to result from a single event, but rather an accumulation of stressful events; these can be ranked – for example, for most children, the death of a friend would rank higher than the death of a pet. 'Additivity' is the idea that the combination of two or more stress-making situations greatly increases the risk of emotional disorder, even though one does not necessarily cause another (Goodyer, 1990). Therefore, tackling just one aspect of stress can have an unexpectedly large benefit. But which comes first? Are the specific events so stressful because of underlying difficulties, so that children become upset about things which would not bother others? Do gifted children, for instance, suffer more stress in their daily lives because of their underlying problem of being different, and so succumb to anxiety about relatively small things?

Taking his cue from his original subject of biology, Piaget (1971) pointed to the principle of homeostasis in mental life. He described intellectual activity as a self-righting system: the mind takes in new information and adapts to it by a feedback process, so that it is constantly evolving from a cumulative build-up of complex and flexible mental 'schemata' (patterns of thought and action). In fact, almost all psychologists agree that the developing mind is far from being just a vessel to be filled. From birth (if not before), a person positively constructs his or her own reality in the self-regulated attempt to keep balance and order, and goes on doing this throughout life. Hence, in theory, an adaptable intellect – one which has been well exercised in retaining balance and working at its most efficient – would also be the most resistant to any ill effects from the problems of daily life. To unbalance such a well-functioning mind would take stronger stimuli than would be needed to upset other minds. Although certain events, such as being hit by a bomb, are clearly beyond intellectual adaptation, some mental activities, such as reflection, imagination, and anticipation, can themselves generate stress, independently of specific input from outside.

At the very heart of the concept of coping with life-strains is the assumption that people can be responsive to the forces that impinge upon them by actively doing something to avoid being harmed. To perform this, they draw on their *resources* – a term which does not refer to what they do, but what is available to them in developing their coping repertoires – whether these are psychological or social. *Psychological resources* are the personality characteristics and expertise that come from experience and practice in life; these help withstand threats posed by events and objects in the environment. They can include healthy self-esteem, an understanding of how to solve problems, mastery of a subject area, or a disposition to move towards other people for help when troubled, whilst others may retreat into denial and escapism. *Social resources* are represented in the interpersonal networks of which everyone is a part; the members of these, such as parents, friends and teachers, are a potential source of mediation and support. Because of this interaction between the personal and the objective aspects of the stress process, scientific attempts to measure the effects of specific stressors are extremely difficult.

However, not all children are equally susceptible to stress, and there are some indications from research that a higher level of intelligence is more likely to safeguard the individual than a lower level. To date, there is no scientific evidence that exceptionally high ability is *of itself* associated with stress and resultant emotional problems, as borne out by Freeman's research (1991). Indeed, it is possible that children with an advanced and wider variety of coping strategies would be better adjusted than their peers, possibly encouraged by a life-history of success. In a longitudinal study of a group whose life circumstances were traumatic, Werner and Smith (1992) coined the term 'resilient' for those children who managed to reach a happy and competent adulthood, compared with their peers who went on to sustained emotional problems. One important feature of the successful children was that they were 'engaging' – able to command the attention of adults in their lives, especially someone outside the immediate family circle. But in addition, the cluster of protective characteristics included an external support system of responsive schools and religion, together with robustness, sociability and above-average intelligence. In accord with that last characteristic, other research has pointed to the stress-reducing benefit of 'cognitive appraisal' – an intelligent awareness present in all mental coping strategies (Lazarus and Folkman, 1984).

In a review of the literature on the contentment and sociability of both gifted and non-gifted pupils, it was concluded that, where there were differences between them, they favoured the gifted (Olszewski-Kubilius et al., 1988). In particular, gifted primary school pupils had lower levels of anxiety, with higher productivity and motivation than their peers; they were also more independent of parental approval, and coped better with psychological problems. In another study, stress in children was compared for gifted and non-gifted groups, using self-reports along with parent and teacher reports (Czeschlik and Rost, 1995). The gifted were found to be socially and emotionally somewhat better adjusted.

Special stresses on gifted children

Yet paradoxically, the gifted do have particular problems and vulnerabilities, and a less attractive picture emerges when looking at the stress levels of extremely high achievers. Although it is recognised that a modicum of anxiety does improve results – if only in specific circumstances such as exams – some children who were extremely successful academically, particularly in the sciences, were found to be creatively inhibited because of the narrow focus and pressure of their school education (Freeman, 1991). In a survey of comprehensive schools, Turner (1986) found that a 'work-restriction' norm was common, even among high-ability pupils – getting away with doing the minimum amount of work was widely applauded. Hence, an ambitious child in a predominantly working-class comprehensive school probably has to study at home in secret if he or she is to avoid the label 'swot' and the disapproval of schoolmates. Strangely, it was quite acceptable to come top of the class, as long as you are not seen to work for the results. Most of the pupils believed that intelligence is innate and that to work hard is to interfere with nature. Those who did work hard and remained popular achieved this by behaving stupidly in class from time to time, such as shouting out silly answers, or contradicting the teacher; or they sometimes diverted attention to someone who was an even bigger 'swot'.

Even when children are selected for more intense, highly structured schoolwork because of their ability to achieve top grades in examinations, the dilemma for educationalists is that development of a playful, creative approach to their work and general outlook may thus be stunted (Cropley, 1995). Children are sometimes pushed into competing for advancement in a race in which their other abilities may wither, each working too hard in too narrow a field, as well as sacrificing leisure interests. Too much competitive striving can build up a ruthless, aggressive outlook.

The emotional vulnerabilities of the gifted come from other people's attitudes to them and from inappropriate education – two overlapping and interacting factors. In their exceptionality and sensitivity, they sometimes construct extremely complex, inhibiting psychological barriers to relationships with others, at times almost encouraged in this by adults who believe that they are too clever to be normal in that respect. In fact, it has even been claimed that the special stresses of gifted adolescents can make them vulnerable to depression and at risk of suicide (Yewchuk and Jobagy, 1991). As with all children, emotional problems usually inhibit school success and social relationships.

The gifted are sometimes under extra pressure from parents and teachers to be continually successful, so that their opportunities to find out about life at their own pace and in their own ways can be drastically reduced – a situation complained about in a follow-up of 1964–1968 Presidential Scholars in the USA (Kaufman, 1992). Although the ex-scholars continued to do well, they often described how they relied on academic skills to provide them with an identity. Gifted youngsters may also be stressed by the unrelenting pressure of teachers who expect a high level of learning and reproduction of information, leaving them feeling intellectually unexercised. It depends how pressure is applied, though. Nathan Milstein, the distinguished pianist, was not noticeably talented as a boy, hated his lessons, but was forced to practise for long hours by his mother, with little thought for his emotional development – which nevertheless appears to have proceeded normally (Milstein and Volkov, 1991). But others under a pressured 'hot-house' regime, such as William Sidis (Wallace, 1986) and Jacqueline du Pré (Easton, 1989), were emotionally damaged by it.

All long-term studies on the development of exceptional talent have shown the cumulative effects of the interaction of family attitudes with the gifted child (for example, Bloom, 1985; Heller, 1991; Freeman, 1991). Problems can arise because a child's gifts produce reactions in others which may be too difficult for the child to adjust to. For instance, in a family where the child is considerably more advanced than the siblings, the parents may become confused so that they act inconsistently and perhaps produce an exaggerated rivalry in the siblings. Or a child may be brighter than his or her parents, who may offer too much reverence to their exceptional youngster, feeling that the normal structuring of good parenting is inappropriate for such a 'genius'. Abilities may develop at different and extreme rates, which can bring difficulties of developmental co-ordination and balance (Terassier, 1985), or parents may also raise their all-round expectations, even though the child is only gifted in a specific area. Since no child can perform at a high level all the time, both fear of failure and a sense of failure and of disappointing the parents will inevitably occur, with possible poor emotional consequences. The parents of gifted children can themselves have resulting emotional problems, either feeling inadequate, or trying to gain social advantage from living vicariously through their child. Whatever problems already exist in the family, these can sometimes be intensified when there is a gifted (and hence unusual) child present (see Freeman, 1993b).

The gifted suffer particularly from stereotyping and its expectations, though the distorting myths vary considerably with the social environment – whether they are unable to make friends of their own age, or whether they

are perfect at everything. However, Post (1994) found that, with few excep-
tions, his 291 world-famous men were sociable and 'admirable human
beings ... Genius as a misunderstood giant is one of the many false stereotypes in this field' (p.31), although the artists rather than the scientists were
somewhat more likely to have emotional problems. Often, a superior moral
dimension is implied in the definition of giftedness. There are programmes
in the USA for 'gifted leaders', for example, which are based on the assumption that the gifted are better fitted to guide the less gifted (though the
natural leadership skills of the head thief of a gang are not included). The
alternative view – that the gifted are morally weaker than other children –
sometimes appears in unscientific work: 'There is evidence that some of
these [gifted] children who are not recognised and supported become
involved in crime and turn to delinquency' (George, 1992, p.viii). In fact,
there is no evidence for this at all. A typical problem created by others
happens when an intellectually gifted child (usually a boy) becomes known
as the 'little professor'; at 6, this reputation can bring glory, when classmates
look up to him and teachers and parents find him 'cute'. Even though it is
perhaps a little worrying that he may have no friends, this is only to be
expected because of his superior thinking abilities and consequent boredom
with others. But by the age of 15, having developed few social skills and
being afflicted with the normal problems of adolescence, the gifted youth
may, in fact, have been well prepared for a life of loneliness.

Unfortunately, the quality of research work on gifted children varies
widely, and the subject attracts many self-styled 'experts', all of which
contributes further to the problems of stereotyping and false ideas about the
gifted. The major problem is the imprecise definition of giftedness, but
in addition, there are biased samples, such as those selected for gifted
(summer-) schools, so that there is often a lack of any comparison groups.
This is true for retrospective studies of outstanding adults (Radford, 1990), as
well as other problems of trying to identify the social forces of the time.
Strong concern with stress in 'profoundly gifted children' was described in
an Australian longitudinal study of just three young subjects. They were
seen as typically gifted, being subject to stress because of their giftedness and
without any friends because they had 'nothing in common except the
accident of chronological age' (Gross, 1992, p.114). But if the gifted child
invents stomach-aches to avoid school, the giftedness cannot be said to have
caused the problem, unless this behaviour is compared with that of other
children, preferably in the same class. In a four-year investigation of talented
teenagers (Csikszentmihalyi et al., 1993), learning to invest in difficult tasks
was found to be very dependent on social support: the stronger the support,
the more developed the skills. Schools were much less effective than parents
in this, because of their curriculum requirements and failure to engage the
interests of the pupils.

Educational stress

A primary educational problem for the gifted involves gaining access to an appropriate level, breadth and speed of learning. It is not only the content of what they receive which is important, but the manner in which it is presented, which may not be in accord with their style of learning or interests. Like all other children, the gifted need *consistent* challenges, and may spend too much time 'filling-in' with exercises, because they have finished before the rest of the class. High achievers are often 'rewarded' by extra work. Normal classroom work can be too easy for them, so that they may develop poor work habits, in the sense of organising themselves.

Underachievement at school in the highly able student is most often due to the same emotional causes as in other children, such as disruption at home (Butler-Por, 1993). But in addition, in a mixed-ability class, in an attempt to make friends, such youngsters may try to hide the evidence of their intellectual exceptionality, in order to be like the others. Gifted girls in mixed-sex schools often have this problem, and may feel that, if they show their brilliance, they will not be seen as feminine. In fact, gender has emerged as the single most salient variable across many studies (see Freeman, 1995). Gifted females respond differently to educational experiences, and often underestimate their abilities (Reiss and Callahan, 1989). However, mentoring and action to improve self-esteem have been found to be effective in promoting a more realistic presentation of girls' abilities (Arnold and Subotnik, 1994). Intellectually gifted girls have been found to be more depressed than equally able boys, possibly due to the conflicts and stresses surrounding female success, although they were happier than less able girls (Luthar et al., 1992). Yet it is virtually impossible to behave in a gifted (especially a creative) way without distinguishing oneself from one's schoolmates. What is more, functioning at an unnaturally low level all the time can also result in stress and anxiety.

Youngsters who have a heightened perception of what could be done can set themselves impossible expectations. An example is a young child whose hands are not big enough to span an octave on the piano. She knows what it should sound like, but has to make a little jump between thumb and little finger, rather than bringing both down together, so the sound is wrong. Perceived failure is thus inevitable, which can discourage enthusiasm for learning and performance. Without adequate emotional support, even the most potentially talented child may simply give up.

Boredom is a particular problem for the gifted child with a curious mind in a normal classroom, who may try anything to relieve this unpleasant experience (Freeman, 1993a). Boredom is not apathy; it is a real emotion, which comes from low spirits and from the anger of frustration. It drains energy, and is demoralisng and maladaptive to the individual. It can also become a habit, developed in early childhood, so that an individual learns to expect it, and so interprets too many experiences in that way. Gifted children, like any others, need the enjoyable stimulation of variety, as well as the excitement that can come from playing with ideas; but when lessons are too easy, they lose the satisfaction of tackling and resolving problems. To compensate, they may deliberately provoke disturbance, either in their own minds or among others in the classroom, just to taste the spice of stimulation.

Although some youngsters have specific gifts and thus can see their career route quite clearly, perhaps in music or physics, there are others who seem to be able to do almost anything to a high standard. For them, vocational problems can be severe: by school-leaving age, one highly talented boy in Freeman's (1991) sample had acquired degree-level music qualifications, but he also had top marks in science. His dilemma was whether to study music or medicine. After great anguish, he decided to take the science option and did qualify, but he found little in common with his fellow medical students, and now, as a practising doctor, still yearns for his music.

The Freeman research

A 14-year follow-up study of both gifted and non-gifted children throughout the UK was unique in its deep interviews with all the sample in their homes, as well as with their families and teachers (see Freeman, 1991). A major aim was to find out why some children were seen as gifted, while others – of identical measured ability – were not. The 70 target children aged 5 to 14 (from a population of 5,637) had been presented by parents as gifted, without independent tests, to the National Association for Gifted Children (UK). Each was then matched with two control children for age, sex (two-thirds boys) and school class (N=210). But although one of the controls was matched exactly for general intelligence by the Ravens Matrices, the second was taken at random in that respect. Because of the sampling procedure, the intelligence scores were skewed from IQ 98 to high, with 82 children at IQ 141+ on the Stanford-Binet test, although the scores on these two types of intelligence test were not always equivalent (Freeman, 1983). The children were also given a wide variety of tests, and their environmental circumstances were rated.

Those who had been labelled 'gifted' (whether they actually were so or not) had far more behaviour problems than those of equal ability who were not so labelled, at 1 per cent level of significance. High-level achievement was associated with access to adequate learning material and tuition, as well as with parental involvement and example. The possession of IQ 140–170 was not found to be related to stress and consequent emotional problems, which were instead associated with other difficulties in the child's life, for which a variety of reasons were offered, such as school discrimination against the child. The idea that gifted children were bound to be 'odd', and accordingly unhappy, was found to be common among both parents and teachers, who sometimes seemed almost to encourage it. Followed up ten years later with the same methodology, although many of the emotional differences between the groups had gone, there were still distinct differences in the young people's behaviour and outlooks associated with family dynamics: those from unhappy homes remained more disturbed, and the children's gifts (manifest or not) were sometimes blamed for this. Pressure to achieve highly was sometimes placed on youngsters who were not gifted, which imposed stress, though the gifted youngsters often exerted considerable pressure on themselves.

The effects of pressure

There are parents from every walk of life who want their children to fulfil the parents' own dreams, and who are prepared to spend great amounts of energy and money to make these come true. A handful of the gifted young people in this sample seemed to be squeezed to the last drop of effort to do better and better. For some, the fact that they could achieve the results without much obvious effort wasn't good enough; they had to be *seen* to work for them. For such parents, a 'good' school always 'stretched' their children and had a record of high examination success. But some youngsters, for whom the pressure had accumulated to an insupportable level, suddenly opted out of school just before the end; they were making their bid for freedom, with some unhappy results of disillusion and lost direction.

It was not always possible to tell where the pressure came from – how much from the young people themselves and how much from outside. For example, one boy's determinedly achieving parents were both scientists, who said they simply could not imagine a family where people were concerned about the arts. The same was true of the boy himself, who spent all his time and energy on scientific study, to achieve the highest possible marks and early entry to university, but to the clear detriment of his emotional development. He knew that his self-esteem depended on the academic rewards he could present to his parents, and was worried that, one day, he would no longer be able to keep up the pace.

A characteristic profile of a pressured, highly-achieving pupil emerged from this research. The high achiever, who was more likely to be a boy, accepted the goals and authority of his academic institution, which were reinforced by higher esteem from the teachers and support for this high-standard work. He carried this acceptance of authority over into non-school activities, such as leisure pursuits. Some saw university as a rather nicer form of school, where they worked very hard, were occasionally inspired by the teaching, but were usually unaffected by the wider opportunities there. Most of them had chosen to study science. They had few, if any, friends, and they were also somewhat short of imagination.

Pressure from home was also imposed on young people who were seen as gifted but who, in fact, were not. As these children could not live up to this ideal, it promoted a remarkable variety of excuses from the parents, as well as some depression in the children.

When a decision was made to accelerate gifted children to a higher class at school, both parents and teacher had acted sincerely, in a way that seemed right to them at the time. However, none had asked any of the children what they themselves would have preferred, and for 16 of the 17 accelerated children in this sample, normal growing-up problems had been exacerbated by this act. For example, talking to the whole family about how it had affected them, both children and parents explained how difficult it was to cope with the younger child wanting to stay out as late as the older ones in the class. The one boy who was very pleased with the situation was tall and mature for his age. One father said of his son: 'I felt sorry for him; they were men and he was a boy.'

Being gifted and different

Throughout the study, those in the top 1 per cent of the IQ range said they felt 'different'; this was at a high level of statistical significance (1 per cent). For most, the gifts which made them different were a source of pride and pleasure, just like any other blessings of nature. Parents saw the feelings of difference as starting very early in life, and suggested that the negative aspects were due to other people: 'Alison was always top at school, so some parents counted their child's order in the class as though she wasn't there. She used to keep her hand down in the class, things like that, so she wouldn't stand out.' But those less happy aspects usually diminished with growing up and with the increased freedom to choose companions more like themselves.

Since the first part of the study, several of the young people had lost contact with one of their parents through divorce, the boys appearing to be more adversely affected than the girls. Two gifted boys had been suddenly deserted by their fathers at educationally crucial times; in one case, this was without warning, just three weeks before his school-leaving examinations. In both cases (according to the mothers), the boys' outstanding abilities appeared to have played the catalysing role in those events; the fathers had left just when the boys both had their greatest need of security and were also about to display evidence of their exceptional abilities, which were greater than those of their fathers. In spite of their emotional shock, both boys excelled.

Of the 8 gifted young people (out of more than 100) who said their gifted-ness was an insuperable barrier to making relationships, all but one were male; their loneliness could be terrible, and by the time of the follow-up study, the outlook from this point of view seemed bleak for them. Like 'academic ostriches', they had buried their heads in their studies, thinking that the rest of the world could no longer see them.

Anna Freud (1937) was the first to describe the workings of the psychologi-cal defences behind which some of these intellectually gifted youths were hiding. In her view, protective emotional strategies are formed when people are confronted by an anxiety-provoking situation and unconsciously avoid seeing it. The favoured psychological defence of some of the gifted, especially boys, was to hide behind a façade of scholarship, so withdrawing from the normal process of learning to make relationships. The psychological defence systems they had built against anxiety had started in early childhood, and at times seemed to be encouraged by their parents, who took this as one of the mythological 'signs' of giftedness. Over the years, their withdrawal behind those barriers had become extreme in a few cases, cutting them off from emotional contact with others. Six young men had gone so far as to almost sever any intimacy with other people – a process which they all blamed on being gifted. One explained: 'The only school activity I was involved in was the Christian Union. I also worked in the school library for six months as an assistant. I had a really good time then.' Another had moved ever further into isolated study, cutting down on his feelings towards other people, and moving closer and closer towards the stereotype of the gifted scientist: peering down microscopes by day and returning alone to his room at night. His father approved of the solitary research work his son was doing, as he said it suited his character.

Yet measured ability, no matter how high it was, did not affect the major-ity of these gifted young people in their ability to have good relationships, and many were exceptionally empathetic. In fact, those who said they used empathy consciously and frequently in their daily lives were most often the intellectually gifted; quite a few of them used this ability to help others.

Specific help for the gifted

As a method for developing the very highest levels of expertise, formal education is of limited value. Education authorities, whether governmental, local, or the schools themselves, can help the highly able pupils fulfil their potential and achieve emotional balance by recognising and providing for their special needs. A policy for these pupils could include, for example:

Pupils

- Counselling and vocational guidance from counsellors who are aware of the stresses and needs of the gifted, such as the problems of acceleration and possible alternatives, such as enrichment or part-time withdrawal. Counselling techniques for the gifted are those normally practised with children, including good counsellor–parent communication (see Milgram, 1991). Vocational guidance cannot begin too early.
- Out-of-school activities for highly able pupils from different schools in the area, such as weekend activities, competitions, or summer camps, where they can meet and relax with others like themselves.
- A system of mentoring – this means that a carefully selected adult with particular expertise takes a special interest in a highly able youngster. The child may, for example, work alongside a scientist in a laboratory doing original research. This often has additional positive emotional effects.
- Facilities for enrichment in education, including extra courses, specialist advisers, and events for gifted pupils. If the level is high, pupils can be self-selecting, avoiding the hazards of selection by test identification.
- A school atmosphere in which attention and provision for the highly able is a normal and natural aspect of differentiated education for all pupils.

Teachers

- Pre-graduation and in-service courses on the education of the highly able – this could include, for example, concern with learning styles and skills, as well as self-understanding of personal biases. Teachers should be provided with a bank of curriculum enrichment materials and teacher-education materials in a resource centre, open outside school hours.
- Recognition that the creative approach is also a questioning, playful approach. Encouragement of the youngster's motivation to reach the highest levels possible, with honest feedback about the pupil's emotional development.

Conclusion

An environment in which the exceptionally able child can prosper all-round must be balanced – allowing the child to spend enough time with other people to develop good social relationships, developing interests outside study areas, and taking part in school and other community activities (Wagner, 1995). This needs recognition and the will of parents and teachers to make sure that the non-examinable side of their pupils' lives is adequately promoted.

The real differences between the gifted and other children lie in their abilities, not in their emotional stability. This means that their greatest needs – just as for all other children – are for security, an appropriate education, and the life-chances to make the most of their potential. But highly able children do need some extra emotional help in the form of adult awareness and support, both because of the power of their own learning potential and because of other people's reactions to it.

It is important for teachers and parents to avoid the temptation to put too much emphasis on the development of scholastic abilities at some cost to emotional needs. Gifted youngsters respond well to teachers who will work *with* them, rather than *for* them; to teachers who are concerned with the structure of their learning and their ability to cope as individuals. For an emotionally balanced life, the highly able do need some exposure to the stimulation of like minds, honest communication, the opportunity to follow their interests to the extent that they want to, and acceptance as all-round people.

My final conclusion is positive – that the gifted who grow up in homes in which there is emotional peace and security will be at least as able as any others to adapt to society and take advantage of whatever provision for learning is available.

References

Arnold, K.D. and Subotnik, R.F. (1994) 'Lessons from contemporary longitudinal studies', in Subotnik, R.F. and Arnold, K.D. (eds) *Beyond Terman: Contemporary longitudinal studies of giftedness and talent*, Norwood, New Jersey: Ablex.

Bloom, B.S. (1985) *Developing Talent in Young People*, New York: Ballantine Books.

Butler-Por, N. (1993) 'Underachieving gifted students', in Heller, K.A., Monks, F.J. and Passow, A.H., *International Handbook of Research and Development of Giftedness and Talent*, Oxford: Pergamon Press.

Cropley, A. (1995) 'Creative intelligence: A concept of "true" giftedness', in Freeman, J., Span, P. and Wagner, H. (eds) *Actualising Talent: A Lifelong Challenge*, London: Cassell.

Csikszentmihalyi, M., Rathunde, K. and Whalen, S. (1993) *Talented Teenagers: The Roots of Success and Failure*, Cambridge: Cambridge University Press.

Czeschlik, T. and Rost, D.H. (1995) 'Sociometic types and children's intelligence', *British Journal of Developmental Psychology*, No. 13, pp.177–89.

Easton, C. (1989) *Jacqueline du Pré*, London: Hodder and Stoughton.

Freeman, J. (1983) 'Environment and High IQ – A Consideration of Fluid and Crystallised Intelligence', *Personality and Individual Differences*, No. 4, pp.307–13.

Freeman, J. (1991) *Gifted Children Growing Up*, London: Cassell.

Freeman, J. (1993a) 'Boredom, high ability and underachievement', in Varma, V. (ed.) *How and Why Children Fail*, London: Jessica Kingsley.

Freeman, J. (1993b) 'Parents and families in nurturing giftedness and talent', in Heller, K.A., Monks, F.J. and Passow, A.H. (eds) *International Handbook of Research and Development of Giftedness and Talent*, Oxford: Pergamon Press.

Freeman, J. (1995) *Highly Able Boys and Girls*, Nene: National Association for Able Children in Education.

Freud, A. (1937) *The Ego and the Mechanisms of Defense*, London: Hogarth.

George, D. (1992) *The Challenge of the Able Child*, London: David Fulton.

Goodyer, I.M. (1990) *Life Experiences, Development and Psychopathology*, Chichester: John Wiley.

Gross, M.U.M. (1992) 'The early development of three profoundly gifted children of IQ200', in Klein, P.S. and Tannenbaum, A.J. (eds) *To Be Young and Gifted*, Norwood, New Jersey: Ablex.

Heller, K.A. (1991) 'The nature and development of giftedness: A longitudinal study', *European Journal for High Ability*, No. 2, pp.174–8.

Kaufman, F.A. (1992) 'What educators can learn from gifted adults', in Monks, F.J. and Peters, W. (eds) *Talent for the Future*, Maastricht: Van Gorcum.

Kennedy, S., Kiecolt-Glaser, J. and Glaser, R. (1990) 'Social support: Stress and the immune system', in Sarason, B., Sarason, I. and Pierce, G. (eds) *Social Support: An Interactional View*, New York: Wiley.

Lazarus, R.S. and Folkman, S. (1984) *Stress, Appraisal and Coping*, New York: Springer.

Luthar, S.S., Zigler, E. and Goldstein, D. (1992) 'Psychosocial adjustment among intellectually gifted adolescents: The role of cognitive-developmental and experiential factors', *Journal of Child Psychology and Psychiatry*, Vol. 33, No. 2, pp.361–73.

Marjoriebanks, T. (1992) 'Ability and personality correlates of children's abilities and aspirations', *Psychological Reports*, No. 17, pp.847–50.

Milgram, R.M. (ed.) (1991) *Counselling Gifted and Talented Children*, Norwood, New Jersey: Ablex.

Milstein, N. and Volkov, S. (1991) *From Russia to the West*, London: Barrie and Jenkins.

Olszewski-Kubilius, P.M., Kulieke, M. and Krasney, N. (1988) 'Personality dimensions of gifted adolescents: A review of the empirical literature', *Gifted Child Quarterly*, No. 2, pp.347–52.

Piaget, J. (1971) *Structuralism*, London: Routledge and Kegan Paul.

Post, F. (1994) 'Creativity and Psychopathology: A study of 291 world-famous men', *British Journal of Psychiatry*, No. 165, pp.22–34.

Radford, J. (1990) *Child Prodigies and Exceptional Early Achievers*, London: Harvester Wheatsheaf.

Reiss, S.M. and Callahan, C.M. (1989) 'Gifted females: They've come a long way – or have they?', *Journal for the Education of the Gifted*, No. 12, pp.99–117.

Subotnik, R., Kassan, L., Summers, E. and Wasser, A. (1993) *Genius Revisited: High IQ Children Grow Up*, Norwood, New Jersey: Ablex.

Terassier, J. (1985) 'Dyssynchrony: Uneven development', in Freeman, J. (ed.) *The Psychology of Gifted Children*, Chichester: John Wiley.

Turner, G. (1986) *The Social World of the Comprehensive School*, London: Croom Helm.

Wagner, H. (1995) 'Non-school provision for talent development', in Freeman, J., Span, P. and Wagner, H. (eds) *Actualising Talent: A Lifelong Challenge*, London: Cassell.

Wallace, A. (1986) *The Prodigy: A Biography of William James Sidis, the World's Greatest Child Prodigy*, London: Macmillan.

Werner, E. and Smith, R. (1992) *Overcoming the Odds: High Risk Children from Birth to Adulthood*, Ithaca, New York: Cornell University Press.

Yewchuk, C. and Jobagy, S. (1991) 'Gifted adolescents: At risk for suicide', *European Journal for High Ability*, No. 2, pp.73–85.

6 Children from ethnic minorities

Kedar N. Dwivedi

Introduction

Children from the ethnic minorities are exposed to most of the same stresses that affect children in all cultures and ethnic groups. However, in addition to these general stresses, children from the ethnic minorities can also be exposed to direct or indirect racial prejudice, abuse, discrimination or disadvantage and to the undermining of their identity, self-esteem and culture.

Ethnic minorities in the UK

Nearly 10 per cent of the UK population are from ethnic minorities, the majority of whom live in inner-city areas. However, half of the coloured population in the UK were actually born in this country.

The major settlement and growth of ethnic minority communities in the UK took place in the 1950s and 1960s, and this was actively encouraged by UK employers due to labour shortages. Most of the immigrants at that time came from the West Indies. The population in the West Indies includes many different ethnic groups, among which people of Indian origin are the most numerous, but the migrants from the West Indies to the UK were mainly of African origin, and therefore the term African-Caribbean is commonly used to describe them (Mares et al., 1985; Sontag, 1979; Hiro, 1971; Edwards, 1979; Black, 1989).

'Racism' or 'racialism' refers to practices of unintentional or deliberate racial discrimination and beliefs based on racial prejudice. Prejudice means pre-judging individuals or groups without adequate knowledge, and an unwillingness to change one's views in spite of sufficient factual evidence to the contrary.

Most children, whether from the minority or majority ethnic groups, have to learn to live with ethnic diversity as the 'melting pot' concept of a single culture resulting from the blending of different ethnic groups has to give way to a pluralistic view of recognition and acceptance of differences between various ethnic groups. The multi-cultural approach aims to promote greater understanding between the different cultures and to alleviate inequalities in a multi-cultural society. Ruth Prawer Jhabvala (1987) highlights the issue so well:

> To live in India and be at peace, one must to a very considerable extent become Indian and adopt Indian attitudes, habits, beliefs, assume, if possible an Indian personality. But how is this possible? And even if it were possible – without cheating oneself – would it be desirable? Should one try to become something other than what one is? (p.21)

Most of the immigrant families in the UK have experienced dislocation, cultural shock, loss of informal support systems, restrictive and sometimes humiliating immigration procedures, considerable social and psychological pressures, various forms of social/economic discrimination and an alien and sometimes threatening and hostile culture. A larger proportion of coloured than white people in the UK suffer from social/economic disadvantages, such as poor housing, unemployment, poor jobs, lesser opportunities for education and training, etc. Most social policies tend to ignore minority cultures, and suppress or dismiss cultural variation in the name of 'integration'. At the same time, the word 'disadvantage' can sometimes be wrongly used to imply that the people who are disadvantaged have brought their misfortune upon themselves because of their inadequacy or some kind of inferiority – they are blamed for their situation.

According to Foulkes (1948), we are all literally permeated by the social dynamics of the community in which we live. In a racist society the dynamics of racism is internalised by all its members, and racism, in so far as it is a feature of a society and its culture, will leave its specific imprint on the individual psyche of all its members, black or white, who have learnt racist values, assumptions and beliefs through the language and the culture (Blackwell, 1994).

There is a tendency on the part of most people from the ethnic majority – and even many from the ethnic minorities – to deny, disbelieve or ignore racist attitudes and practices. Unless one has been a victim of discrimination (for example, on grounds of gender, class, age, disability or colour) oneself, or has been emotionally close to someone who has been a victim, it is difficult to fully appreciate what it feels like to be discriminated against just because of the colour of one's skin.

Service uptake

Storti (1989) describes the process that easily leads migrants to withdraw from indigenous people and institutions. Often one expects others to be like oneself but finds that they are not, and a cultural incident then leads to a reaction of anger or fear and prompts one to withdraw. What begins innocently as a self-protective reflex quickly hardens into a pattern of systematic evasion and withdrawal. Agencies such as schools, social services, primary healthcare teams, clinics and hospitals are often irritated by this withdrawal, which prevents some members of ethnic minorities receiving the help they need, but there are also cultural biases in help-giving institutions which are not very conducive to service uptake.

In Western culture, the traditional forerunners of therapeutic institutions were perhaps the priests. A priest came into contact with his clients when they turned to him for help. One had the opportunity to confess in a private, confidential setting with the hope of receiving advice, forgiveness or even punishment, and then felt relieved.

In the East the counterpart was perhaps the guru. The guru's clients stayed with him for extended periods of time, serving him and refashioning their own lives after the examples of the guru under his surveillance. What mattered was not the guru's qualifications, salary or talents in making wonderful speeches, but the way he lived. A guru's life had to be an open book, transparent with purity of conduct, living and practising what he preached.

Maybe because of this cultural heritage, Eastern clients tend to seek an informal relationship with therapists rather than a strictly professional one. This is one reason why, even when clinics employ well-qualified, knowledgeable and dedicated therapists, there is such a low uptake of their services from ethnic minority families.

Another reason for the low uptake of helping services stems from communication problems. Language difficulties and the lack of adequate translation and interpretation services in many help-giving encounters reflect institutional racism. Many instructions and forms of feedback are therefore often completely misunderstood, with very damaging consequences. Often, unwilling volunteers or children from within the family find themselves in the embarrassing position of having to translate and interpret concerns beyond their emotional, linguistic or social capacity. In addition, there is also the issue of differences in styles of communication. Western culture values direct and clear communication, whilst indirect and masked communications are seen as rather substandard and inferior. In the East, on the other hand, indirect and metaphorical communication has been valued as an art form. It is seen as a more mature and sophisticated form of communication

– it creates more space for the possibilities for change and compromises. It generates more options and face-saving opportunities; it activates not only the left but also the right hemisphere of our brains.

Eastern culture puts less emphasis on asserting and expressing one's own opinions and feelings, and more emphasis on understanding and not hurting others. Therefore, indirect and metaphorical communication is seen as a more responsible style of communication, as it allows more time and space for the message to permeate.

White European ethnocentricity

Independence is a cherished ideal in the West. Since the Industrial Revolution, Western culture appears to have placed the greatest emphasis on independence; being dependent is seen as a stigma, a source of shame and a cause of grave social problems at all levels. Therefore, at the family level, parents are at pains to help make their children independent as soon as possible. Teachers, social workers, youth workers, therapists, relatives, parents and the media all try to foster autonomy, individuation and separation; the entire culture promotes this. As a result of this trend, there is now a rising tide of narcissistic disorders (Lasch, 1980).

Eastern family dynamics, seen from such an angle, appears to be rather stifling, primitive and oppressive, as independence is not seen as a cherished goal in Eastern culture. What is valued is dependability, as a developmental goal. At the family level, parents are at pains to create an atmosphere of dependability, so that their children can model themselves upon that and grow up to become dependable and model parents themselves. Babies are therefore subjected to an atmosphere of indulgence, prolonged babyhood, intimate physical closeness, common sleeping arrangements and immediate gratification of their physical and emotional needs (Roland, 1980). From the Western perspective, it is a culture of spoilt children, but it fosters strong bonds and provides an inner sense of security, trust and strength. As separation experiences for very young children are considered unnecessary, there is very little need for transitional objects or commercialised play materials. A professional brought up in Western culture may easily misinterpret this as a situation of deprivation.

Once a foundation of inner security, interpersonal trust and bonding and an inner sense of strength has been established, then there is usually a change in expectation during the latency period. The expectations now are that the growing children will increase their tolerance of their feelings without acting them out or expressing them in a hurtful manner, becoming more and more sensitive to others' feelings, and transcending narcissistic attitudes with the development of an attitude of co-operation and sharing with and caring for others (Dwivedi, 1993a; Walley, 1993).

The sources of stress

In addition to the usual stresses related to schoolwork, family life, physical problems, financial and social problems and life-events, children from the ethnic minorities are also exposed to stresses arising from ethnocentric undermining of their value systems, racial disadvantage, discrimination, prejudice and abuse.

The Campaign for Racial Equality (CRE, 1988) and Troyna and Hatcher (1992), while addressing the problem of racism in schools and racial harassment, describe a number of harrowing incidents. For example, a young man of Sikh origin who has published his moving account was subjected to regular physical and verbal harassment in the seven years that he spent in schools in the UK – even teachers sometimes joined in such disgraceful activities. A young Muslim girl was deeply hurt by being taunted about her Muslim dress by her best friend (a white girl): 'Can't you afford proper trousers? This is not a Paki school.' An 8-year-old boy of Caribbean origin was alleged to have urinated on the toilet floor. Despite the fact that he insisted he was innocent, the teacher made him clean the floor. When the child's father came to the school to complain about this, the police were called to see him off the school premises, the child was suspended indefinitely from school, and finally moved to another school.

As there is a tendency on the part of many people to deny, disbelieve, ignore or even encourage racial abuse, this leaves vulnerable people, particularly children, feeling helpless and hopeless faced with racial discrimination, abuse and bullying in schools, playgrounds and other places (Beliappa, 1991; Dwivedi, 1993b).

The Campaign for Racial Equality (CRE, 1989) have also made extremely helpful recommendations to help eliminate racial discrimination in education. Ross and Ryan (1990) suggest ways of improving the social atmosphere in school playgrounds, where the racist incidents are often initiated. The report of the MacDonald Inquiry (1989) documents the chain of events which led up to the murder of an Asian boy in the playground of his school. The report also identifies factors that can lead to such incidents and ways to prevent them. A Newham Monitoring Project publication (NMP, 1990), based upon ten years of experience, also makes practical recommendations about how schools and local education authorities can respond with effective anti-racist measures. Similarly, a periodical entitled *Multi-Cultural Teaching* (published termly by Trentham Books) is available to help update teachers with a range of multi-cultural and anti-racist strategies for schools. The Home Office (1989) has also issued guidelines for a multi-agency approach to dealing with racial harassment.

The effect on children and their expression of stress

Idioms of distress are determined by one's culture, as culture transmits social values across generations (Sontag, 1979). Cultures can encourage or discourage certain behaviours, offer their preferred interpretations, and influence the presentation of certain problems or their presentational forms.

Communities differ in terms of what behaviour is considered desirable in children (Minturn and Lambert, 1964). Hackett and Hackett (1993) emphasise that screening instruments validated on an indigenous population will need to be reweighted if they are to be applied to an immigrant sample, so that they reflect the patterns of tolerance and stringency unique to that ethnic minority community. For example, a study in Manchester found more stringent expectations in most areas of child behaviour on the part of the Gujarati community. This was based upon semi-structured interviews consisting of 131 questions based on Newson and Newson (1968) behaviour patterns – for example, related to independence, concentration, obedience, aggression, fears, sleep, bedwetting, lying, etc. Hackett and Hackett (1993) noted: 'the more exacting notions of normality in the Gujarati community might lead one to expect more children to be labelled as deviant; in fact the opposite seems to be the case' (p.356).

Children born to immigrant parents in the UK are inevitably exposed to their own communities' norms at home, but also to the norms of the host community at school and elsewhere. This leads to a potential for conflict with their parents (should they exhibit behaviour at home that would be acceptable at school) and/or conflict with their teachers (should they exhibit behaviour at school that would be acceptable at home).

Although there is a very high degree of exposure to stress for ethnic minority children, certain groups of these children have much greater inner strength because of their cultural upbringing, as described above. This can offer some protection against mental health problems. For example, a study in Leicester (Kallarackal and Herbert, 1976) surveyed all children of Indian origin who were in the final and penultimate classes in those Leicester junior schools with pupils of predominantly Indian origin, using Rutter's questionnaires and including 261 boys and 260 girls. A randomly-selected sample from these was then matched with ethnic majority controls and interviewed for further study. The study found that the children of Indian origin were three times less maladjusted than their counterparts (11 per cent and 31 per cent respectively). There was also a higher prevalence of family breakdowns, single parenthood, serious marital problems and prolonged absence of one parent in the ethnic majority children in comparison to the children of Indian origin.

The difference in perceptions between the school and parents regarding ethnic minority children is highlighted by the study of Rutter et al. (1974) of 10-year-old school children in an Inner London borough using Rutter's questionnaires for teachers and parents, and also interviews with randomly-selected teachers and parents. They estimated the prevalence of psychiatric disorder on parental interview as 25 per cent in children from non-immigrant families and 17.5 per cent in children from West Indian families. However, the level of disturbance became markedly different from the teachers' points of view on the basis of teachers' interviews – the estimate of psychiatric disorders in children from immigrant families rose to 38.2 per cent, and in non-immigrant families to 27.6 per cent.

Cochrane (1979) also used Rutter's teachers' questionnaires, and found the rates to be 6.8 per cent for children of West Indian parents, 5.7 per cent for children of white parents, 4.2 per cent for children of Pakistani parents and 3.6 per cent for children of Indian parents. A retrospective study by the Department of Child Psychiatry at the London Hospital (Stern et al., 1990), using an analysis of their case notes, found that children of Bangladeshi origin were markedly under-represented in their referrals in comparison to the local population. They estimated that, in their area, nearly 33 per cent of school-age children would be of Bangladeshi origin, but only 12 per cent of referrals to their department were from Bangladeshi families.

Case examples

Even if the amount of psychiatric disturbance in ethnic minority children is not very high, it is often associated with elements of racism. The following case examples illustrate how racial dimensions compound psychiatric disturbance and its management. For example, Michael's disturbance was compounded by the fact that he had been left by the local authority in the care of a very frail and ailing West Indian grandmother. Nisha, a young woman of Gujarati origin, became suicidal in the context of racial teasing at school and a lack of traditional family support at home. The educational and therapeutic plans for Akram (a child of Bangladeshi origin) did not accommodate the family's cultural and value systems, with psychotic consequences. (The names have been changed to preserve confidentiality.)

Michael

This boy of West Indian origin was referred to our clinic at the age of 14 by his social worker. He had been living with his maternal grandmother, as his own mother had a history of psychiatric illness and was unable to cope with children. Michael's two younger brothers were also accommodated by the social services department in a foster-home.

At the time of referral, Michael was already 5ft 10ins tall and well-built, but he was emotionally rather immature and had a history of asthma. His mother had had several relationships, and was in and out of the local psychiatric hospital. As it was believed that his mother had physically abused him as a young child, he was moved to live with his grandmother, where he grew up. His grandmother had already split up from her husband. Michael had regular supervised contact with his mother but not with his father, who died when Michael was 12 years old. Michael's grandmother was in her sixties at the time of the referral, and had a history of heart disease necessitating periods of hospitalisation, so Michael had to be accommodated elsewhere during such periods.

Michael was referred to our clinic because his grandmother felt that he was behaving in the same way as his mother had when she was his age. The grandmother described to the social worker that Michael was bizarre, anti-social and disobedient. However, our psychiatric assessment did not reveal any clear evidence of any psychotic symptoms. He co-operated with individual and then group therapy sessions, overcame his anti-social behaviours (lying and stealing) and managed to share many of his feelings. He also built up his self-confidence and self-esteem, and his caring nature became very evident in the group. However, the relationship with his grandmother remained strained. He found her to be over-anxious, restrictive and demanding, whilst she found him careless and inconsiderate. She worried about his spending most of his time in the company of youngsters who tended to get into trouble.

This situation had been compounded by the fact that Michael's care had been left to an ailing and frail grandmother (without much support) who had suffered several heart attacks and, in fact, depended upon Michael as a carer. In addition, he had very little contact with any other West Indian friends or relatives.

Nisha

At the time of her referral, Nisha, a girl of Gujarati Indian origin, was 16 years old. She was the youngest of five sisters; both her parents and two of her sisters were in Kenya, but the other two sisters and herself came to the UK. Out of the two sisters in the UK, one was married and settled but the other had a boyfriend that her parents did not approve of. Nisha was living with this sister so that she could attend school in the UK.

Nisha began to find racial teasing and bullying at school very difficult to cope with. As she became very interested in a boyfriend, the relationship with her sister became very strained and hostile, which culminated in Nisha taking an overdose. Her difficulties were compounded by her isolation and the loss of her supportive network. She had already felt that her parents had been disappointed in her because, having had four daughters, they were hoping for a son.

Akram

Akram was the second of seven children from a family of Bangladeshi origin. He was born while his parents were still in Bangladesh, and grew up normally up to the age of $3^1/_2$ years. He then contracted meningitis, which impaired his speech and hearing. The family came to the UK when he was 4 years old, and he was given a hearing aid and attended the partially-hearing unit of a mainstream school. He was recommended for residential education, but could not handle separation from his family, and the family felt unable to let go of him either. He then continued to attend the partially-hearing unit. His communication and other skills remained extremely rudimentary, and as the family moved house and began to involve him in a religious Muslim healing ritual, he became very agitated and started exhibiting psychotic symptoms.

There appeared to be a conflict between the value systems within the family and the institutions relating with the family, with the result that he did not receive adequate training in communication and expression. The stress of the move and being caught between the pressure from the family system to participate in religious rituals on the one hand and the transmission of paranoid perceptions of such rituals by the helping agencies on the other precipitated the emergence of frank psychotic symptoms.

Conclusion

Thus, children from the ethnic minorities are exposed not only to the same stresses that affect other children, but also to additional stresses due to institutional or individual, direct or indirect racial prejudice, discrimination and abuse. However, many ethnic minority groups are able to continue the practices of their child-rearing culture that strengthen the protective inner strength. In spite of this, many ethnic minority children remain vulnerable to various stresses due to their enormity and the gradual or sudden loss of their protective cultural practices and support networks.

Acknowledgement

I am very grateful to Karen Spring for her repeated word processing of this material.

References

Beliappa, J. (1991) *Illness or Distress? Alternative Models of Mental Health*, London: Confederation of Indian Organisations (UK).

Black, J. (1989) *Child Health in a Multi-Cultural Society*, London: British Medical Journal.

Blackwell, D. (1994) 'The Emergence of Racism in Group Analysis', *Group Analysis*, Vol. 27, No. 2, pp.197–210.

Cochrane, R. (1979) 'Psychological and Behavioural Disturbance in West Indians, Indians and Pakistanis in Britain: A comparison of rates among children and adults', *British Journal of Psychiatry*, No. 134, pp.201–10.

CRE (Campaign for Racial Equality) (1988) *Learning in Terror: A survey of racial harassment in schools and colleges*, London: Campaign for Racial Equality.

CRE (Campaign for Racial Equality) (1989) *Code of Practice for the Elimination of Racial Discrimination in Education*, London: Campaign for Racial Equality.

Dwivedi, K.N. (1993a) 'Emotional Development', in Dwivedi, K.N. (ed.) *Groupwork with Children and Adolescents*, London: Jessica Kingsley.

Dwivedi, K.N. (1993b) 'Coping with Unhappy Children who are from Ethnic Minorities', in Varma, V.P. (ed.) *Coping with Unhappy Children*, London: Cassell.

Edwards, V.K. (1979) *The West Indian Language: Issues in British Schools*, London: Routledge and Kegan Paul.

Foulkes, S.H. (1948) *Introduction to Group Analytic Psychotherapy*, London: Heinemann (reprinted 1983, London: Karnac).

Hackett, L. and Hackett, R. (1993) 'Parental Ideas of Normal and Deviant Child Behaviour: A comparison of two ethnic groups', *British Journal of Psychiatry*, No. 162, pp.353–7.

Hiro, D. (1971) *Black British, White British*, London: Eyre & Spottiswoode.

Home Office (1989) *The Response to Racial Attacks and Harassment: Guidance for the Statutory Agencies – Report of the Inter-Departmental Racial Attacks Groups*, London: Home Office.

Jhabvala, R.P. (1987) *Out of India*, New York: Simon and Schuster.

Kallarackal, A.M. and Herbert, M. (1976) 'The Happiness of Indian Immigrant Children', *New Society*, No. 26, February, pp.422–4.

Lasch, C. (1980) *The Culture of Narcissism: American Life in an Age of Diminishing Expectations*, London: Abacus.

MacDonald Inquiry (1989) *Murder in the Playground: The Report of the MacDonald Inquiry into Racism and Racial Violence in Manchester Schools*, Manchester: Longsight Press.

Mares, P., Henley, A. and Baxter, C. (1985) *Health Care in Multi-cultural Britain*, Cambridge: Health Education Council/National Extension College.

Minturn, L. and Lambert, M.M. (1964) *Mothers of Six Cultures: Antecedents of Child Rearing*, Chichester: John Wiley.

Newson, J. and Newson, E. (1968) *Four Years Old in an Urban Community*, London: Allen and Unwin.

NMP (Newham Monitoring Project) (1990) *Racism and Racist Violence in Schools – Ten Years of the Newham Monitoring Project*, London: NMP Publications.

Roland, A. (1980) 'Psychoanalytic Perspectives on Personality Development in India', *International Review of Psycho-analysis*, No. 1, pp.73–87.

Ross, C. and Ryan, A. (1990) *Can I Stay in Today Miss? – Improving the School Playground*, Stoke-on-Trent: Trentham Books.

Rutter, M., Yule, W., Berger, M., Yule, B., Moreton, J. and Bagley, C. (1974) 'Children of West Indian Immigrants – 1: Rates of Behavioural Deviance and of Psychiatric Disorder', *Journal of Child Psychology and Psychiatry*, Vol. 15, pp.241–62.

Sontag, S. (1979) *Illness as Metaphor*, London: Allen Lane.

Stern, G., Cottrell, D. and Holmes, J. (1990) 'Patterns of Attendance of Child Psychiatry Outpatients with Special Reference to Asian Families', *British Journal of Psychiatry*, No. 156, pp.384–7.

Storti, C. (1989) *The Act of Crossing Cultures*, Intercultural Press.

Troyna, B. and Hatcher, R. (1992) *Racism in Children's Lives: A Study of Mainly White Primary Schools*, London: Routledge/National Children's Bureau.

Walley, M. (1993) 'Empathy and Pro-social Development', in Dwivedi, K.N. (ed.) *Groupwork with Children and Adolescents*, London: Jessica Kingsley.

7 Family problems

Anthony Manning

Introduction

This chapter seeks to make a small contribution to understanding children under stress in the context of key relationships developing over time. These children are both the 'worthy', those with whom we can readily empathise in their misfortune; and the 'unworthy', whose behaviour is hard to understand, whose conduct is provocative or even outrageous, and who are generally seen not as suffering from stress, but as visiting stress on others. Given that stress can present in a variety of forms, including anxiety, physical symptoms and anger, it is a useful, overarching concept in approaching work with children and families. It is also easier for people to talk about their experience of stress than it is to face the stigma of having 'family problems'.

In discussing stress in a relational context, I will outline some theoretical principles of systems functioning and explore, with case examples, some 'family problems' which tend to place children in jeopardy of developing acute or chronic stress conditions, and of storing restricted patterns of behaving and relating for adult life. Perhaps what these families have in common is a tendency to close down potential variability and the evolution of new meanings – a state which can either be brought about by attachments which are too loose to provide a sense of belonging, or which are too tight to permit growth. At one extreme, meanings are lost in noise and activity, while at the other, differences have become submerged in repetition, so that beginnings and ends – of a pattern, or indeed, a person – are hard to distinguish. Contempt has bred a kind of familiarity.

In addition, it is hoped to present ways of understanding and helping children who are suffering stress by drawing on ideas from different schools of thought, in order to suggest holistic and integrative approaches to treatment.

The study of occupational stress has been gathering pace for about twenty-five years. The equally important field of family therapy can claim a distinctive history of perhaps forty years, while the psychoanalysis model it was designed to supplant and which was, and remains, essentially a study of the individual, has survived to its centenary.

Each of these models has tended to lay claim to a particular territory: organisations and work groups; the (assumed) pre-eminence of family process, and the interplay of forces, conscious and unconscious, within the individual psyche. Each viewpoint, or set of beliefs, has, for the most part, developed separately with little trade with other 'religions', and more excitement – anxiety – about developing 'churches' within. Inevitably, each theory has contributed ideas – and prejudices – regarding the nature, causation and cure of human problems or distress.

Stress in the context of relating systems

To Freud (1936), the phenomenon of persistent anxiety, or we might say stress, was a problem and a puzzle. He argued that anxieties provoked by external dangers reflected an early childhood prototype of coping with the apparent loss of the loved and longed-for person capable of meeting all of the infant's needs. Freud was greatly puzzled by the enduring nature of disabling conditions of neurotic anxiety:

> in their response to danger so many people remain infantile, continuing to react with anxiety to situations which should have long since ceased to evoke it ... Whence comes the element of permanency in these reactions to danger? ... after decades of analytic effort this problem rises up before us, as untouched as at the beginning. (pp.91–2)

To many systems thinkers, it may be that Freud's 'problem' was that of taking the next logical step into the world of ongoing relationships in the family. His repudiation of his discovery of the sexual abuse of his patients within their families as young children took him away from this whole arena. Therefore, only since about the late 1950s have family therapy approaches considered family relationships as fundamental in both influencing the development of symptoms and in maintaining them interactionally for the protective functions they serve for the family.

Stress often tends to be considered a problem of the individual, yet relatedness and the communication which supports it is at the centre of our experience and being. Within family therapy approaches, problems or symptoms presented by the individual are always considered, at least in part, to be symbolic communications about relationships. Even where family process does not play a primary part in generating the child's distress, family responses, based on prior factors of resilience and flexibility, will play a large part in determining what is done and talked about, and therefore will affect the speed and completeness of readjustment.

Nor should one assume that stress is essentially a negative phenomenon. Hans Selye, working essentially from a biological standpoint, coined the word 'eustress' to give an alternative reading: 'any change in our environment that teaches us to cope, in a better manner, with things in our life' (Selye, 1966). Indeed, in many therapeutic approaches (for example, Milan-systemic, Ericksonian, or even analytic approaches), even – or especially – negative phenomena are valued for their positive intent (Schmidt and Trenkle, 1985).

Such thinking is expressed in common parlance as 'Your body is trying to tell you something.' A family therapist goes a stage further and suggests: 'Your body is trying to tell your family something!'

Throughout this chapter, therefore, stress is considered as a *distress-signal*, an encoded request for assistance for oneself *and* others.

Attempted definition of terms

Coping   It is interesting that scientific attention to breakdown and dysfunction has been vastly greater than that paid to determinants of successful coping or recovery. There is a pressing need for further research in this area, to better understand the differing levels of vulnerability to stresses and trauma, even within a sibling group, and to inform the development of education, support and therapy in this field.

Anthony (1986b) suggests that there are differences which help to explain the reactions of children to severe stress (in this case, terrorising attacks by their own parent, in a paranoid or manic state). These will include: the child's prior state; their competence (for example, scholastic and interpersonal); their vulnerability/resilience, and what Anthony describes as 'the encompassing family'. Of course, the particular child's actual experience of the incident is a crucial factor. The 'prior state' will include predispositions, where an anxiety-prone subject may develop Post-Traumatic Stress Disorder (PTSD), whereas one with a loading towards psychosis may suffer an aggravation of this state, but without PTSD.

Moran and Eckenrode (1992) suggest that relatively resilient adolescent survivors of maltreatment tend to have a strong belief in their personal control of their life circumstances, have a commitment to life, and a willingness to take on challenges. Much depends, however, on the development of self-esteem in early childhood, as a buffer against later shock or trauma. Not surprisingly, therefore, 'long term maltreatment is related to lower levels of protective personality characteristics during adolescence'. Since the failure

of a mother's protectiveness during early childhood – typically in circumstances of severe family dysfunction and economic hardship – is likely to
have a profound effect on the child's self-esteem and on the preparation of
appropriate defences, early intervention with such mothers and families is
vitally important.

In family systems terms, Patterson and Garwick (1994) recommend a
therapeutic approach which addresses three levels of meaning constructed
within the family:

1   situational meanings – specific stressful situations, and the balance
    between demands and capabilities;
2   family identity constructs, such as role structures, routines and rituals,
    and 'meta-rules' about adaptation and change;
3   the family's 'world view' – the extent to which there is coherence as a unit
    about an existence which is meaningful, manageable and understandable.

Similarly, Seaburn et al. (1992) emphasise the function of stories constructed
around chronic illnesses or conditions, such as cystic fibrosis, in influencing
how patients and families function and adapt.

Children   In developmental terms, a child may be considered as a sexually
immature growing person moving from a state of dependency for the
meeting of survival and psychosocial needs to one of increasing autonomy
with maturity. The human infant is characterised by its strong relational
drive, and is generally active from birth in behaviours which promote or
demand attachment behaviours from a parent figure. Children arrive with a
genetic programme of personality characteristics and a range of potential-
ities whose realisation is mediated by immediate conditions of care, the
general environment and chance. Children tend to explore and to seek
novelty, and do so most effectively and safely once a sufficiently secure base
has been established. Through exploration and interaction, internal repre-
sentations of the world and of significant relationships are created which are
incorporated into the self to inform a persisting personal identity and a
'world view' (of others beyond one's boundaries). Major aspects of the self-
concept, derived from emotionally significant early experience, are highly
resistant to change: 'even an unpleasant but predictable world is preferable
to a chaotic one' (Ricks, 1985). Such stable core beliefs from childhood are
powerful factors in subsequent caregiving behaviour.

Child development is continuous, but marked by specific stages, each with
its particular requirements, alongside which run the developmental stages
not merely of other family members individually, but of the family (as a
relatively distinct entity) as a whole.

Legal, political, and sociological criteria may alter the extent to which a person is regarded as a child – for example, the degree of responsibility they are held to possess for their actions, the restrictions on their free choice (or alternatively, the protections afforded them), such as regular attendance at school, and their eligibility to enter employment or the armed services. Crucially, socially constructed viewings of core conditions of the child's being, race and gender will have a potentially large impact on its developing possibilities.

Stress Edwards (1988) offers the following definition: 'Stress is a negative discrepancy between an individual's perceived state and desired state, provided that the presence of this discrepancy is considered important by the individual.' Stress can become a persistent state because of its 'negative impacts on well-being and motivation to minimise these impacts'. Without guidance, people under stress tend to adopt poor or even irrational coping strategies, fuelling the negative spiral. The impact of stress on mental efficiency, mood and behaviour contributes to overpredictable cycles in which there is reduced sensitivity to new stimuli which might otherwise inform a changed perspective.

To a family therapist, the symptoms of the individual will be viewed as potentially representing a condensed, economic version of discrepancies or differences among intimately relating persons. However, Sluzki (1981) suggests that symptoms may long outlive their usefulness, or even that 'many collectively maintained symptoms do not have a discernible triggering conflict at all, and ... result [from] random phenomena that became anchored progressively by all the participants of the collective, as the symptom-maintaining patterns became organising principles for the group'. One might connote this kind of process as a kind of family 'virus', and therefore ask: when this 'virus', with its symptoms of strain, fatigue, misunderstanding and criticism, is finally flushed out of the system, what will you be doing that will make life more satisfying and worthwhile? What did you usually do before you caught the bug? This can prompt some conversations for health at the individual level (mind, body and spirit) as well as at the levels of couple, family and community.

... and where to look for it? In real estate, the three most important features of a property are said to be: (1) location, (2) location and (3) location. Before proceeding further, we should ask where we, as therapists and theorists, would locate stress: at the level of the person, and with the emphasis on physical, or on psychological process? If the latter, we might think in terms of the cognitive framing of experience, or of stress as a symbolisation of unconscious early trauma. Alternatively (or additionally), we might consider stress an interpersonal experience of the group, family or organisation, an expression of its malaise via a distribution of unconsidered

roles, one of which is the sick or symptomatic role, whose main function as a scapegoat is to permit the larger group to escape the realisation of its own distress. At a further level of abstraction, similar thinking might be applied to consider stress as an element of the social and political structure at a particular point in history. Our chosen theory will, of course, determine what we are able to see (Heisenberg, 1971) and how we will attempt to intervene. If a central tenet is that stress arises from the mislabelling of physiological arousal states and environmental cues, we will be disposed to act as educators and coaches to individuals. Alternatively, our beliefs might lead us to attempt family transformation (for example, Minuchin's 'restructuring' or the Milan group's disruption of the game as played (or endured) by families in rigid transaction). Sharing the therapist's invented reality, patients dream Jungian dreams, start to 'see' boundaries and hierarchies (structural family therapy) or to speak in numbers and scales (solution-focused therapy)!

Having said this, it also has to be acknowledged that what therapists actually *do* in sessions does not always closely resemble what they *believe* they do, nor what their chosen model would have them do – the therapy room is, perhaps, another country. It is a mercy that this is so, at least that experienced therapists should work with relative freedom in unique and unkempt situations. Despite our increasing theoretical and technical sophistication, it remains the case that 'the therapist variable' is arguably the most crucial of all, and many would echo Dora Black's (1989) comment that 'The form of the intervention is probably less important than the person doing it.'

It is important, nevertheless, that allowing for individuality – or even idiosyncrasy – should not underwrite 'heroic' and isolated practice. There is an inescapable mutuality of influence between the therapist and the family in treatment and, over time, it may be the professional who comes to be recruited to the family's defensive trance and will need assistance to regain perspective and appropriate distance (Van Trommel, 1984).

What do we mean by 'problem'?   A problem exists when fixed meanings close down perception, cognition and performance, restricting achievement and preventing self-transcendence. A problem state is a trance of a limited, repetitive and monologue-confined world. No news is bad news. In discovering, utilising and encouraging the transfer of client competencies (O'Hanlon, 1991), and by provoking consideration of unfamiliar or forgotten possibilities (for example, Tomm's 'reflexive questions'), the 'shock of the new' is introduced.

A therapist, by extension, is primarily an opener: contrast the doctrine of the salesman, whose every action is geared to closing, where the intended outcome is known from the beginning. Watching for forgotten patterns, skills, rhythms and cadences, the therapist offers an invitation to at least a few steps of a new dance.

What do we mean by family (therapy)?   A dominant debate at this point in the evolution of the family systems paradigm is that between the concept of social organisation based on role structure, and the notion that 'systems can be described as existing only in language and communicative action' (Anderson and Goolishian, 1988, p.375). These authors suggest that the former theory leads to 'the genesis of problems [being] placed on the social system superordinate to the one expressing the deviance'. Essentially, this is viewed as a diagnostic and prescriptive approach, with the therapist as expert, reifying the family as an object of treatment, and as such, a reworking of the old medical model with more patients in the room.

In contrast with this layered socialisation model, Anderson and Goolishian (see also Andersen, 1987; Tomm, 1988) propose a fluid and evolving model of shared language, creating 'shifting communities of meaning (including families) to which we belong' (p.377). Similarly, Dell (1985) suggests that 'social systems (such as families) are distinctions which are drawn by the observer when he or she distinguishes an organised pattern of interaction'. The stance of a therapist within such a conceptualisation is radically different: he or she is collaborative, a learner whose expertise is as an 'architect of dialogue', establishing the richness of multiple meanings of what is said, and enabling space for the unsaid to emerge. To update Shakespeare, albeit at some hazard to the poetry: 'there is nothing either good or bad, but languaging makes it so'.

At a mundane level, this debate between the definite and the emergent, the dead and the quick, as it were, can seem puzzling, if not absurd. We all have a pretty good idea of who is and is not in our family, and if pressed, might even talk about how power and influence operates.

We could acknowledge that other families work differently, especially where there is a cultural difference – but those families, too, know about boundaries and hierarchies and structure and ritual – and these things matter to them. I remind myself that this fascinating, maddening debate is not new, as the following Zen Buddhist story will illustrate (Reps, 1971):

The Stone Mind

Hogen, a Chinese Zen teacher, lived alone in a small temple in the country. One day four travelling monks appeared and asked if they might make a fire in his yard to warm themselves.

While they were building the fire, Hogen heard them arguing about subjectivity and objectivity. He joined them and said: 'There is a big stone. Do you consider it to be inside or outside your mind?'

One of the monks replied: 'From the Buddhist viewpoint everything is an objectification of mind, so I would say that the stone is inside my mind.'

'Your head must feel very heavy,' observed Hogen, 'if you are carrying around a stone like that in your mind.' (p.71)

Science itself is rooted in conversation, as Heisenberg (1971), the atomic physicist, attests in his autobiography. Beyond even the discussion and interpretation of experiments are the shared imaginings of the realms where classical observational science cannot travel. In the age of relativity, the co-involvement of objectivity with subjectivity, the observer with the observed, became a new and intriguing problem. Heisenberg records Einstein's thoughts on the matter from a personal conversation: 'It is the theory which decides what we can observe ... [and] it is no longer possible to make predictions without reference to the observer or the means of observation.'

The unusual activity which is therapy

Therapy is an unusual – and risky – social activity. 'In Erving Goffman's scheme of things, society is only possible if people generally refrain from challenging the questionable statements of others' (Jones, 1990). Yet an archetypal therapy scenario places a therapist pursuing change together with a family invested in stability-with-symptoms! The irresistible force meets the immovable object, and something's got to give – and it may be the effectiveness of the therapy system, as the therapist's beliefs undergo subtle transformation. As Jones explains: 'it is relatively easy to induce ... uncharacteristic behaviour ... under circumstances such that the power of the induction is unrecognised or underestimated'. When this occurs, people have a tendency to recover internal consistency by reasoning that, since the surprising viewpoint was arrived at in an apparently free-choice situation, they must have believed this all along! Jones goes on to talk about the 'autistic conspiracy between ingratiators [loosely one who employs strategies to gain influence over another person] and target persons ... which predicts shifts in the self presenter's private beliefs that make them more consistent with his or her public statements'. It may be, therefore, that in situations of high expressed emotion and fatigue, the therapist starts to believe the counter-paradoxical prescriptions intended for the family, and this may explain his or her aroused emotion in joining the family's irritation with some unhelpful or depriving outsider.

Some principles and values in family systems approaches

A family therapist may be considered as a process consultant, whose task is to assist in making sense of the patient's difficulties in the outside ('real') world, in relation to issues of family growth, belonging and separateness, within a meaning system about that particular family's journey through life. Within this context, a range of 'treatments' can be utilised in this endeavour, including psycho-education, anxiety management training and various forms of group therapy. In adopting this approach, the therapist models safe and effective parenting – being positive, pro-active, logical, respectful, able to consider individual needs, recognising everyone's fundamental desire to belong and to feel significant. There is a genuine fascination with how this particular family does things, and where it, and its members, are trying to get to. Therefore, the symptom will be addressed both in terms of its protective function in helping to achieve protective goals – for example, of people staying close and avoiding distress – and in terms of its blocking function in preventing growth and change and moves towards other desires.

A family systems perspective on helping troubled children is in tune with the times. Herbert (1993) points out that the Children Act 1989 implies a 'focus on systemic (that is family orientated) assessment and interventions designed to help parents/care givers to be more responsive, effective, self-reliant and confident in the care and management of their children ... [stimulating] change in families that are "stuck" in self-defeating, unproductive and growth inhibiting patterns of living'.

Such work is in keeping with the local authority's general duty 'to promote the upbringing of children [who are in need] by their families, by providing a range and level of services appropriate to those children's needs' (Children Act 1989, Section 17(1)).

It is important to outline some key principles underpinning this view of living systems. Much fuller accounts can be found elsewhere (for example, Walrond-Skinner, 1981; Jones, 1993; Hoffman, 1981):

1 Systems are 'wholes', with an identity, some shared sense of meaning and a boundary to distinguish them from 'the crowd' or 'other systems'.
2 A system is not understandable by meeting each of its members (even together), but by observation or immersion in its interactional process – its life and meaning becomes more than the sum of its parts. Nevertheless, individual differences make a powerful difference – for example, Herbert (1993) lists a range of 'inborn attributes' of a child's personality, including: 'very fidgety' versus 'relatively still'; 'adaptable to change' versus 'easily upset by change'; 'loud and intense crying reactions' versus 'more moderate reactions'.
3 Systems develop and change over time, negotiating a balance between keeping things recognisably and controllably 'the same' (a myth, given time and biological imperatives of development) and too much chaos and change. A family functioning in the former fashion would be viewed as having a rigid interactional style and set of rules, denying its members the identity and individuality which would challenge the myth, whilst the latter, a chaotic or disorganised family, would have

little core with which individuals could identify as a moral or meaning-ful system. (Figure 7.1 gives a simplified description of these differing styles and their impact.)

4   There are fairly distinct life-cycle stages and associated tasks (which are modified by social and economic forces: for example, in times of want, the privileges of adolescence may be enjoyed by the few) which affect the whole family, not merely individuals. Developmental stages are potential points of growth or of crisis for families, which can fail to adapt to a new set of needs and get 'stuck': a slip of the tongue by Campbell and Draper's (1985) 'Michael', aged 18, speaking of his powerful mother, neatly makes the point: 'she influenced us from day one and what she is, we are ... I don't know what she's ... what I'm gonna do when she's gone.'

5   Therapists entering systems need to adapt to their particular ecology and style in order to introduce new ideas and information effectively,

RIGID		OK TO OPTIMAL FUNCTIONING		CHAOTIC
Intensely enmeshed: defensive cohesion at the expense of individual members	Pained but coping	Relatively open, able to negotiate, can deal both with need to belong and need to individuate	Pained but coping	Loosely connected individuals with little affectional involvement or sense of duty towards one another

Notes: To use a sports analogy (football), an extreme-end rigid family is all team, no stars: they let very few goals in with their stifling defensive formation, and their encounters are often stalemate 0–0 draws. Their creative players become very inhibited and frustrated. They are not good to watch. It's no good telling them to ease up and express themselves: the last time they tried it, the system broke down and they lost heavily. Expression within the system needs to be encouraged, remembering that they are very suspicious of too much individuality (prima donnas!), emphasising safety and what they already do well.

An extremely chaotic family, on the other hand, is all stars and no team: kick-and-rush boys' soccer, exciting to watch, especially the arguments amongst the players, and likely to win, or lose, 10–4. They need an experienced, firm and organising coach who will slot them into the positions that best suit their abilities and teach them to compete together against other teams, rather than individually against each other.

Figure 7.1   Family styles and their impact

avoiding the risk of the encounter being alien and therefore dismissed, or at the other extreme, *too* comfortable to perturb its slumber (Andolfi et al., 1983, pp.15–20). These are the dilemmas of the therapists who discover themselves to be stuck 'outside' (like an alien) or 'inside' (like a neighbour popping round), and unable to make a difference.

6 Persisting symptoms or problems are understood as being to some degree system requirements, even though there may be individual vulnerabilities or even genetic loadings. In extreme situations, the therapist is challenging the 'game without end' which the family find themselves compelled to conduct, with the 'patient' or 'problem person' immutably at the centre of their existence: flexibility, growth and individual difference may have been sacrificed on the altar of apparent unity and an artificial absence of conflict (Andolfi et al., 1983). To Bateson (1972), symptoms arise as a defence when a person is unable to make sense of incongruous messages (for example, when words signifying affection fail to make a 'whole' with non-verbal qualifiers, such as eye contact and body language). The subject has the dilemma of knowing which part of the message to respond to: the difficulty, as it were, of knowing which is 'figure' and which is 'ground'.

7 Families tend to come to therapy when the stresses associated with maintaining the old order against the inevitability of change have escalated to a point where an individual and the family system face breakdown (Heavey, 1990, p.160).

8 The constricting power of labels and attributions is challenged to allow new possibilities to emerge. To the Milan school of family therapy, this was a fundamental challenge to the 'tyranny of linguistic conditioning' (Selvini-Palazzoli et al., 1978) which defines a situation or a person's possibilities for all time. Such descriptions include, of course, psychiatric and other diagnoses. In a session, a systemic therapist would be more likely to comment that A shows a sad expression when X happens or when she notices B act towards C in a particular way, rather than to say that she was, or seemed, 'depressed'.

9 It can be argued that perhaps the most fundamental 'constricting' labels relate to gender, race and children's rights. Some of family therapy's own assumptions and 'blind spots' in some areas are now being challenged (Perelberg and Miller, 1990; Goldner, 1988). It is important to consider, for example, the largely culturally-determined differences between men and women in entering a counselling situation, and in what they expect once there (Lewis and O'Brien, 1987). The history of misguided assumptions based on racial stereotypes and the abuses of official power thereby licensed, even in the 'caring professions' (for example, mental health; childcare), should serve as a reminder that quite severe psychopathologies can develop and persist in whole

cultures, let alone families. If the unexamined life is not worth living, then the unexamined culture or society is not worth living in.

10   Systems do not begin and end with the family. First, it is essential not to lose sight of the individual who, in turn, is constantly involved in a number of relating systems – mind–body (Griffith et al., 1989); conscious and unconscious processes (Laing, 1960), etc. Next, it is important not to treat the family as a 'thing', for as Laing and Esterson (1964) put it: 'It is immensely difficult not to subject unwittingly our human reality to such conceptual mutilation that the original is lost in the process.' Finally, families themselves differ in their structures within – and certainly across – cultures, and function in relation both to the times they live in (for example, dominant scientific, social and religious themes and beliefs) and to supra-systems (including public policies) to a large extent governing freedoms and opportunities. The 'times' will, of course, inform the functioning of the supra-systems: interpretations of the differences between women and men, for example, will feed through into regulations about freedoms, access to education and employment, etc.

11   'Accidents will happen': from particle behaviour to accidents of evolution, life is always to a greater or lesser degree uncertain. This 'Uncertainty Principle' is important for therapists, in recognising with humility that, while they can help prepare the ground, they can never fully determine what will grow in it. This is part and parcel of the excitement of relative freedom, and many therapists, particularly of the strategic schools, have played with this unpredictability, utilising their confident uncertainty to provoke the unexpected. After all, as the poet Theodore Roethke (1968) put it: 'In hell there is no change.'

In what follows, there is no intention to suggest watertight categories, perhaps merely an attempt to find some useful distinctions in describing contexts of stress affecting children.

Emotional and psychological abuse and parenting failure

It is increasingly, and belatedly, being recognised that parental mistreatment can affect the child's development and expression of feelings as well as a range of mental and cognitive faculties. The parents of such children, and those who fail to thrive, may have experienced considerable hardship and misery throughout their own lives (O'Hagan, 1993).

Such children are often viewed and described negatively as 'difficult' and 'unrewarding'. A particular child may be 'chosen' as the container of bad emotions.

In Greek mythology, certain newborn babies were exposed on the mountain to die: these infants, like Hercules, presented a threat, and if they survived, might come to be extremely powerful, in contrast to their initial abject weakness. Whilst no ordinary scapegoated child can possess the capabilities of a Hercules to confront his or her undoubted labours, he or she may assume significant powers as they endure the burdens of their parents' repudiated characteristics. Dare (1993) has written about such children, selected and positioned from the earliest days for particular opprobrium.

Coercive parenting styles may contribute to disordered behaviour, including aggression. It has been noted (Patterson, 1982) that parents of aggressive children tend to lack consistency, fail to associate punishment clearly with transgression, give in to demands when the child counter-attacks, generally fail to offer supervision and monitoring, show little warmth, share few pleasant activities and do not teach or demonstrate the difference between right and wrong effectively or show children what to do or not to do in a given situation. Eventually, stresses can become overwhelming, with verbally abusive and violent tactics increasingly the first resort. As the situation escalates, they are certainly living in what Ausloos (1986) described as 'eventful time', with a lack of reliable structure contributing to conduct disorders, educational failure, employment difficulties, etc.:

> In families with chaotic transactions, information circulates but it is just noise; it cannot be retained, stored or remembered. Events succeed one another incessantly and throw everything into disarray. (Ausloos, 1986)

Barker (1993) suggests that infants who display a disorganised style of attachment behaviour, lacking a coherent strategy for coping with separations and reunions, and showing unusual forms of behaviour suggesting fear and confusion towards the parent, are likely to be the products of chaotic families.

However, emotional and psychological abuse is not perpetrated only by a single 'type' of family; the unfathomable double binds of the more enclosed and rigidly organised families described by Laing contribute to existential confusion and the possible development of psychotic forms of illness.

In working with such families, it remains important to attend to the specific difficulties of the child. Some children have temperamental and learning difficulties, often from the earliest times, although an adverse environment will certainly worsen their plight. They are characterised by inattentiveness, being easily distracted, and impulsiveness; they are easily over-aroused and frustrated, constantly restless, have difficulty in deferring rewards or adapting to new situations, and have marked problems with social skills and friendship development. Sensitising parents to the child's difficulties and helping them to achieve an awareness about the difference between non-compliance and inability is essential in building success (Goldstein and Goldstein, 1992).

Dadds (1987) suggests that a thorough assessment of child behaviour problems requires an analysis of four sets of factors:

1 *Intrinsic factors* within the child (the child's biological status): babies arrive with their own temperaments – some are irritable and hard to comfort, others may be unusually placid. The mother's (or primary carer's) mood state, and therefore ability to respond appropriately to the infant's needs, is, of course, crucially important, but the pre-existing state of the individual baby has often been underestimated.
2 *Factors acting upon the child*: these include parenting styles and practices, and the impact of separation and divorce, disrupting known parameters, with new and often complex structures ('blended families') providing further tests both of loyalty and flexibility.
3 *Factors within families*: these include the personal adjustment of family members, the marital adjustment of parents, and the interactional style of the family. These are the areas which tend to preoccupy family therapists.
4 *Factors acting upon families*: these include the broad range of social, economic and political influences – socio-economic status, housing, community facilities (crucially, schools, childcare facilities and medical care), the availability of extrafamilial support, State intervention and access to the law to redress wrongs. Added to these are unpredictable events or catastrophes, whether of natural or human origin.

Since these broad categories seem to be useful in designing a balanced assessment, both in the child protection field and beyond, Figure 7.2 gives an example of a family session summarised using this format.

Professionals working with children who have suffered abuse have many dilemmas, both ethical and pragmatic. They have to take a position about the best interests of the child, and may therefore have to act decisively; at the same time, the Children Act 1989 exhorts them to work in partnership with parents in preserving family life whenever possible. The principle of paramountcy ('that the welfare of the child is the paramount consideration in proceedings concerning children', DoH, 1991) gives a seductive impression of clarity, whereas the situation on the ground is inherently tense, and professionals have somehow to balance the rights of the family with the needs of the child, both as a particular exercise and as a general one, on behalf of society, following concerns about emergency removals of large numbers of children where sexual abuse was suspected, in the Cleveland area of northern England (Butler-Sloss, 1988).

As well as the difficulty in remaining clear about who is one's primary client, thought needs to be given to the differences between a formal reporting role and one's usual therapeutic one: otherwise, ideas of neutrality and circularity, and of indeterminate futures, are liable to collide with issues to

Factor	Observation	Possible Intervention
The Child/Young Person	6-year-old mixed-race boy, mother from Antigua, father Scots, half-sister of 16. Very watchful at first: later moving from one uncompleted activity to another. Seems clumsy, and mother blames him for constantly breaking and spilling things. Mother notes pre-session improvement in co-operation.	Note improvements and give her credit. Reframe 'wilfulness' as usually inability or stress. Developmental check. Liaison with teacher. Need for extra help, socially and with reading?
Parenting/ Other Influences	Alternately coercive and permissive, based on collapse. Mother complains about *her* mother 'taking over'. Father left about 2 years ago; ex-wife gives him a list of instructions (diet, etc.) for contact visits, which he ignores. Disputes about money and property.	Mother has good range of skills, but current problems of overload and poor self-esteem. Work on assertiveness. Talk with her solicitor. Subsequent session with mother and *her* mother.
Family and Marital Adjustment and Interaction	Mother says husband 'changed completely' on marriage. Confusing dominant–submissive style. When matters seemed to be more settled, she discovered his extensive gambling debts. Broke up with subsequent man-friend 6 months ago, although he 'still visits occasionally'. Daughter, Gina, extremely reserved and studious. Mother's brother served a prison sentence for robbery.	Exploration of history and relationships via genogram (including Gina's different history: what happened to her father and his parents?). Use family cohesion questionnaire?
External Factors	Risk of house being repossessed, debts. Mother gave up law degree course during family crisis. Her father currently in hospital (local) following a second stroke. Mentions racism, but plays it down. Thinks teacher this year not firm enough with Ben. Sends *her* mother to deal with any problems/meetings in school.	Mother agreed to work out figures and write to building society this week for an appointment. Referred to welfare benefits team for further advice. Discuss race/gender issues more explicitly. Meet teacher and Special Educational Needs Co-ordinator in school later?
General Comments	A family with a lot of resources, but rather embattled and isolated at present. Mother very anxious about children (especially boys?) going out of control – tries too hard to be in control, then gives up, exhausted.	Slow the pace down. Needs lots of encouragement, play and humour.

Figure 7.2 Summary of a family session

do with unequal power, expert status and the court's need for statements and predictions that are definitive. Nevertheless, such problem areas need to be resolved as far as possible to provide balanced professional advice on what is most likely to help a child. Black et al. (1989) remind us that: 'Sometimes legal intervention can be more effective than many years of treatment.'

The worker may also sympathise with the parent, whose abusive or neglectful behaviour may result from a similar, or worse, history, added to by current situational stressors. In being called to give evidence in the interests of the child, the worker risks being seen by the parent as hostile and abandoning: collusion to avoid such stress is even more dangerous, as such overidentification with the unloved child-in-the-adult both ignores the realities of adult responsibility and may overlook the real child entirely. The worker's 'objectivity' will be influenced by a range of factors: training and experience, support and supervision, the availability of alternative resources to help families, and the prevailing views of abuse (and, indeed, of social workers) which inform a climate of optimism (in which the emphasis is on co-operative work with families, with few children removed) or of pessimism (with greater use of compulsory powers) (Dingwall, 1989).

There will be further anxieties about the availability of suitable placements, the difficulties of achieving permanency, the complexities of future contact arrangements, and the lack of therapy and support services post-adoption, contributing to the risk of further disruption, rejection and possible abuse of the already psychologically damaged child. Some adoptive families are challenged beyond endurance by children who have not only suffered repetitive loss, but also may never have known what Laing and Esterson (1964) refer to as the 'all-over' quality of care which produces a lively and hopeful self. Indeed, the child's original self-negating defence in an oppressive situation may have become a basic structure for coping with the world, leading to impoverishment across a range of mental and emotional functions, including the capacity to experience joy. However benign and tolerant the substitute care may be, without therapy to address the punitive and uncaring internal images stored at the core of the self, such a child may remain as if a stranger in a strange land, starving amidst plenty, repaying kindness with provocation and withdrawal, until the adoptive parents, perplexed and exhausted, give out the hostility the child seems to crave, or give up the ghost entirely.

O'Hagan (1993) gives a number of detailed accounts of assessments where children may be suffering 'significant harm' through emotional and/or psychological abuse. Thorough preparation and good team support are essential in this demanding and potentially stressful area of work, where there is so much at stake for both child and parent.

Case example: My needs or yours?

Marion and her three daughters came to us for a court-mandated assess-ment of her parenting capacities, the children coming to sessions from their foster-homes.

Marion was a large, quite impressive figure, endearing and even a little refined at times, whilst capable of scarlet-faced tirades delivered in the booming voice of a sergeant-major. When this happened in sessions, the therapists seemed much more alarmed than any of the children. The eldest looked around fleetingly, before carrying on pouring imaginary tea, pre-occupied and precise.

We met Marion's mother, Enid, once, and went to ask her to join us in mid-session. She had her arm around her daughter in the waiting room and was baby-talking her into taking a Valium to 'calm herself down'. Enid's style was rather that of the *grande dame*, unable to comprehend her daughter's moods, mistakes and lifestyle, and particularly her choice of men. Enid's speech was littered with caustic condemnations as she explained the problems of her life, and particularly the obstacles she had faced in her battle to save her daughter from herself. How she had been up against it! Marion had been so unaccountably hyperactive and violent as a child, and the people in the outside world had made her worse; the children bullied and taunted her, the teachers failed to teach her ('I even had to do that myself') and the Head would not take Enid seriously, even when she insisted that there was something wrong with Marion's brain. The career of the long-suffering and overwrought rescuer persisted into the present, and every time Marion foolishly tried to break away, she loyally fell flat on her face.

Marion depended on her mother, who could help her out practically and financially, and despised her at the same time, resenting her interference and her compulsion to give good advice. Marion boasted that she wouldn't take advice, even (especially?) good advice: this was a sign that the other person was trying to dominate you! Sometimes when she was depressed and the kids were getting her down, she would go for a drink or two and get chatting. Friendly, girlish and vulnerable, she was not a good judge of men, tended to throw herself – and her children – into new relationships and, predictably, was hurt and deserted many times. One cohabitee was dis-covered to be a Schedule One offender. Whenever she owned up to her latest mistake, her mother would welcome Marion back into the fold, the daughter's contrition and relief mixed with rage and rebellion.

Whilst all the children were stressed in different ways, Anna was in par-ticular difficulty as the 'family scapegoat'. Anna – aged 5, in the middle between an older boisterous sister and a younger one, wide-eyed and doll-like – was always in the wrong, and in the wrong place. Whilst her sisters had 'accidents', Anna only had 'on-purposes'. When things went wrong for her mother – social workers getting heavy or a boyfriend backing away – it was obvious who had started it, or at least tipped the balance. There was indeed increased chaos if Mum was preoccupied with a boyfriend and maybe about to ask him to move in, since she lost sight of the children because of the stars in her eyes. One might even suggest that their 'uproar' protected both mother and children from the consequences of another rash decision. And yet Anna came to be seen as special, gifted with second sight, and admired for her resilience. (Her oppositional way of coping and strong will were, in my view, protective personality features (Moran and Eckenrode, 1992) in these circumstances, though her behaviour might more usually be seen in a negative light.) At times her mother had some awareness of the process: 'When I look at Anna, I see myself as a child.'

The dilemma comes to be whether the child will win through, hardened in the fire, or will be damaged or destroyed in, as Dale (1992) put it, 'the catastrophe of replica situations', and where this battle should be fought out – in the person of the new child, or in the reintegration of the damaged and rejected child-within-the-adult?

Marion was a character one could sympathise with, and yet whose personal needs were so overwhelming. Her moods changed unpredictably. She would do the wrong thing just to be cussed. When she felt let down, she would cut the offending party out of her life – and unfortunately, this applied to her children too. Her demanding and dramatic style had previously led to her being asked to leave a group treatment programme. Her 'personality disorder' and parenting behaviour indicated a poor prognosis.

Marion's own self was still so graspingly hungry that she was unable to put others' needs first, although she could see, for short periods, that she should.

Parenting is not a one-way street, of course. One might therefore ask how able, or willing, the parent is to watch and listen, learn and be changed by the experience of relating to a child as an authentic and unique other. In Anna's case, her 'news' could not be celebrated by her mother, since it triggered her own recall of unmet needs, fuelling anger with the world, and competition with her own child.

Sadly, but inevitably, Marion lost her bid to regain her children, who were freed for adoption.

The family system organised around alcohol

The children of alcohol- or drug-dependent parents are liable to disadvantage and risk in a number of areas, depending on the nature and degree of their parents' problem. The 'problem', in turn, will be a combination and interplay of factors to do with the drug(s) of choice, the individual concerned and the relational context and functions of the drug use. Briefly, factors to do with the drug itself will include:

- the inherent properties of the drug (for example, stimulant, depressant, hallucinogen);
- its physical effects or side-effects, including acute and longer-term health risk (and here we need to consider the paraphernalia of ingestion, especially shared needles and the risk of transmission of HIV; drug use during pregnancy and its effects on the unborn child; foetal alcohol syndrome, etc.; the dangers of children having access to alcohol or drugs in the home, and indeed the known risks of passive smoking);
- the degree to which the effects on the user can be predicted, particularly for illicit supply, where there will often be doubt about contamination (for example, from the manufacturing process, or to 'bulk up' supplies for extra profit for the dealer chain), and even the identity of the substance; the mood, expectations and circumstances of use of the subject, and difficulties associated with chaotic or multiple drug abuse;
- the legal classification and associated penalties of conviction for possession, use or supply;
- prevalent attitudes to the use or abuse of a particular drug;
- the availability and cost of the substance, which, together with its inherent properties, will influence the money and time needed to support continued use, in turn affecting lifestyle around employment, crime (including prostitution) and subculture affiliations.

Secondly, factors to do with the individual will include:

- the gender of the individual (for example, safe drinking limits are likely to be considerably less than those advised for most women and for most men);
- the ethnicity of the user, which may at times influence drug choice and distribution networks, as well as the policing of particular groups and areas;
- the employment opportunities available to the individual, which may make a major difference as to whether the drug use is recreational or a phase, or alternatively, whether it becomes part of a hopeless and deteriorating condition. A worthwhile job can provide – as well as money – responsibility, stability, structure (even at the most basic level of having to get up in the morning), purpose, ambition to progress, and the opportunity to contribute something, thereby promoting self-esteem and the good reputation of the family;

- the psychological characteristics of the individual, including impulsiveness or ability to delay gratification and work for success; the ability to make judgements; the willingness to take risks; the level of need for peer approval, and crucially, self-esteem, personal autonomy and willingness to accept responsibility.

Stanton and Todd (1982) suggest that problematic drug use, often starting during adolescence, is likely to signify: 'an intense fear of separation experienced by the family in response to the addict's attempts at individuation … The drug … permits him to simultaneously be both close and distant, in and out, competent and incompetent, relative to his family of origin.'

Thirdly, the relational context of substance abuse is a key area to understanding both the evident and the more subtle influences on a child's life and development:

- Persistent problematic drug or alcohol abuse is likely to portray both chronic self-esteem difficulties (Crafoord, 1980) rooted in family-of-origin distress (including significant losses and a history of neglect or abuse) *and* current relationship processes. Instead of mutuality and growth, starkly complementary styles evolve, giving a semblance of stability by, for example, alternating nurse–patient or martyr–delinquent roles, in a constantly repeated and restricted interpersonal game. Children play roles within this 'game' and store patterns for future relationships. Beattie (1989) refers to this process as 'codependency', whereby beliefs and rules of transaction are absorbed which inhibit the development of mutual, loving relationships. The learned pattern is based on power, where the addiction becomes a third party in a relationship based on denial and projection.
- The family may come to be stigmatised in the neighbourhood, and the child at its school, contributing to problems of self-esteem, achievement and attendance, and increasing the risk of developing alternative lifestyles – at one extreme, based on acting out and delinquency, and at the other on a relatively isolated caretaker role.

For these reasons, children of parents or carers with 'addiction' problems carry a loading for stress, both acute and chronic, based on:

1 the general quality of attachment (particularly early attachment, if the adult problem was active at that time);
2 associated life-events, legal, medical and socio-economic;
3 the absorption of a repetitive, limiting and often destructive relationship style.

Case example: From drink to the brink

Joel's outbursts, and particularly two alarming incidents of lashing out at other children on the mildest provocation, led first to his temporary exclusion from school, and then, following an urgently-convened meeting, referral to our service.

Getting the family to a session took three attempts and the assistance of the doctor who had previously provided the mother with a good deal of support. Even then, the family attended without the father because, we were told, of a job interview which had suddenly come up. We decided to proceed and interviewed, to a large extent, around the theme of control and loss of control in the family. This was coherent with the presenting problem around Joel's behaviour but also allowed access to parenting patterns and revealed long-standing drug and alcohol use by both parents.

Descriptions of key family members often contained opposites in terms of their individual characteristics: for example, father was portrayed both as 'an irresponsible, womanising drunk' and as a 'lovable mixed up victim of circumstances'. In keeping with this was the family's tendency to distribute roles based on someone being a caretaker, and someone being sick or incompetent. We asked about this process, as it affected adult relationships; how it changed from time to time; how the children were drawn in, tried to help or distance themselves, and came to take on supporting or provocative roles. All of this was part of a dramatic script where the family was always about to explode, but never did; where someone was on the verge of reform, or at least decision, never achieved, and where the day-to-day unpredictability of life was part of a deeper-level pattern of predictability and repetition.

Part of the sustaining of this system came from the powerful secondary gains associated with drinking, including the opportunity to show caring and forgiveness, times of raucous humour, and occasions of sexual release after episodes of violence: 'you are locked into your suffering and your pleasures are the seal' (Cohen, 1966). Similarly, Liepman et al. (1986) comment on the 'gains' of the increased collusive closeness of the non-drinking spouse and the children, and of the expression of forbidden feelings, otherwise blocked, during a drinking episode, concluding that: 'without family therapy, most families would suffer serious side effects if the alcoholic were to stop drinking permanently'.

Subsequent work, influenced by Onnis (1988), focused firstly on improvement of self-esteem in the parents, through the medium of parallel individual sessions which reviewed personal history and examined strengths along solution-focused lines; secondly, a reframing of the drug and alcohol problems in terms of the control games ('see if you are strong enough to make me stop'; 'help me feel strong by having a problem to help with, or failing that to justify my suffering'), and thirdly, enhancement of parenting competence as a prelude to attempts to help the couple to restructure their relationship on more satisfying lines.

This work is continuing and is inevitably difficult. Research (Rutter et al., 1990) suggests that presumed 'genetic' factors 'may manifest in terms of temperamental futures (such as sensation-seeking and poor impulse control) that pre-dispose to both anti-social behaviour and alcoholism'. Therefore, helping parents to act competently and set appropriate limits contributes to more ordered conduct in the child and may therefore be presumed to contribute to reducing the risk of subsequent alcoholism. This is not to underestimate the functions of alcohol as a drug, and the likelihood that, in the vast majority of cases, those who are addicted will fail to learn controlled drinking and may need to enter a rigorous treatment programme, such as the 'Twelve Steps' approach, aimed at achieving abstinence and personal/spiritual growth (Fishman, 1988).

A fourth major area of work focused on Joel himself, largely based on 'play', helping him to complete tasks and thereby to see and value his own productions. Parenting work assisted in this area too, in helping the parents to create time and space, to make clear and fair rules, and to prevent fighting disrupting completion and enjoyment.

Dealing with loss and associated change through death, divorce and disaster

A family's capacity to adjust to major life transitions of these kinds and achieve a new functional system is a major indicator of their previous flexibility and coping strengths, as well as the availability of support systems. With very complex emotional and practical readjustments to make, families and their individual members are vulnerable to stress, and can get stuck at particular points in the working-through process. Bowlby-West (1983) detailed 12 common homeostatic adjustments, ranging from anniversary reactions through family secrets to pathology, including the expression of the same physical symptom that caused the death.

In the field of divorce, a child who suffers a severe conflict of loyalties (Klosinski, 1993) may attempt to cope by trying to support the weaker parent: in extreme situations the child is effectively psychologically maltreated, with anxiety and guilt feelings induced to draw the child on to one parent's side, and used as a messenger or spy, abducted or illegally retained, or forced to witness criticism and physical abuse between the separated parents. Such children need a period in therapy using non-verbal (for example, drawings) as well as discussion-based methods to get in touch with their own feelings and conflicts (Markham, 1990). Children may have 'lost' their parents for a long time during the gradual, or concealed, disintegration of the marriage, and the more withdrawn child, in particular, may store up the impact of their loss, to be triggered in the event of a subsequent traumatic incident or loss (Ayalon and Flasher, 1993).

Children's lives may be assailed by catastrophes of natural or human violence. It is essential that sensitively-conducted debriefing is available to them as soon after the event as possible, and subsequent practical and care arrangements plus individual and family therapy can be arranged. This whole area of enquiry is only recently emerging as a priority, and therefore services are often absent or patchy, and much remains to be done to plan and resource appropriate and well-co-ordinated services. Failure to do so can leave children whose worlds have blown apart, vulnerable to subsequent breakdown (Terr, 1990).

Johnson (1989) describes three sequential phases of response to the impact of trauma: recoil, reorganisation, and a path of restabilisation which will leave the family functioning either significantly better or significantly worse in terms of patterns of intimacy, affection, communication and trust:

> We are struck ... as we get to know more troubled families by the way that these qualities of resilience, adaptability and sheer ability to love and care for each other may be enhanced and dramatised by a family tragedy. (Hendriks et al., 1993, p.138)

Relatively cohesive families can certainly help their members to cope on a number of levels: cognitively (in redefining the person's behaviour during the crisis); emotionally (in bolstering the person's self-esteem, whatever his or her current difficulties may be); in terms of affiliation (belonging and social integration), and instrumentally (chores and services). Thereby, the effects of exposure to trauma are mitigated (Solomon et al., 1987).

As with normative crises, families with prior conflict patterns and communication problems may be relatively poorly equipped to cope. Similarly, families may get stuck at a particular readjustment stage. For example, Anthony (1986a) comments on the tendency of parents and children to huddle together after a disaster, with parents clinging to children 'as if they were talismen'.

As Wallbank (1992) has pointed out, the loss suffered by a child through the death of a family member may not be acknowledged in letters and cards of condolence: the norm is to comfort the principal griever. Children are often excluded from funeral rites, usually from motives of compassion, but are thereby deprived of an opportunity to begin to accept the reality of what has happened. Still more perplexing, some children are told nothing, or half-truths, or plain untruths, to 'protect them from the truth', particularly if the truth is unpleasant – for example, suicide, an accidental drug overdose or an accident while drunk.

After this immediate phase, there may be many further changes to adjust to: financial struggles affecting what the child may now do; moves of home and school; anniversaries and other reminders; new partners for the surviving parent, perhaps with their children in tow. To get through this time intact and still trusting, what Wallbank calls 'oases of private comfort' within the family – or with a teacher, family friend, or therapist – are needed.

Case example: In the midst of life ...

Tim was already on the run from life – thrown out of his secondary school in his third year, and involved in juvenile crime – when his mother committed suicide. Only a few weeks earlier, she had tried to seek a reconciliation with Tim's father, but, having taken her back twice before, he could not face a third attempt.

The presentation of this case unfolded according to this schema: first, an uncooperative and anti-social boy threatened with exclusion from school (the reasons for his behaviour were unknown) who provoked strong and, in the main, punitive responses. Second, a marriage that was falling apart, and where there had been prior separations; father's explanations were vague and fogging, with talk of long hours and worries about a failing business. He apologised for his difficulty in putting things into words, especially feelings, which were his wife's domain. She had enough feelings for the two of them, with her extra-marital affairs, her constant talk of her childhood, and her depressions which would sideline her for weeks at a time, often when he needed her most. Third, the father's own childhood deprivation and delinquency as a teenager, including a spell in borstal, emerged.

Much later, Tim's older sister, the achieving and coping one, was revealed also to be carrying psychological pain, expressed through obsessions and depressive episodes.

Tim's own behaviour, increasingly reckless, wrecked his capacity to think or feel anything. Thereby he communicated his feelings of hopelessness about saying anything worthwhile which could make a difference. Tim's offer of himself as a bigger problem than his parents' marital difficulties failed to reunite them.

Soon his mother was dead, from suicide by drinking bleach. In the aftermath, the father's incipient depression surfaced, while Tim's shaky grip on self and reality became increasingly evident. A psychotic form of illness replaced the 'mindless' acting-out through which he had expressed his desperation in former days.

A uniting framework for therapy for this adolescent and his family was built around a view of isolated and confused people, the self-containers of their woes, seeking different, and sometimes desperate, means of escape – through sensation, or distraction, or running away – in the world, or in the mind. The psychotic episodes themselves could be considered re-enactments of unbearable separations and confusions; signifiers of former times when distress was palpable but no one could break through into meaningful communication. Psychotic states also had helpful features, keeping Tim in a containing situation, and reducing the risk of acting-out, and of suicide.

The opposite of 'escape' is, perhaps, running towards, embracing, engulfment, and exploring this shadow side opened up areas of need, which included some memories of feeling cared about, and of caring and attempting to protect others.

Secrets, myths and repeating scripts

It can be suggested that both symptoms and myths arise in the attempt to deal with incongruence and secrets embedded in the life of the family. These families are trying to protect a 'repudiated reality' (Anderson and Bagarozzi, 1983).

Some families maintain powerful secrets (obscuring from themselves even the fact that there is a secret), betrayed only by an ultra-cautious style of relating to outsiders and mysterious forms of behaviour, rituals, compulsions and obsessions. The children of such families are often enigmas, viewed as 'different' by their peers and teachers, often intelligent and perceptive, but somehow unreachable.

The function of secrets appears to be to reinforce shaky boundaries, preserving the illusion of family (and personal) integrity, both currently, and in the past. Secrets held collusively can form powerful myths, within which different individuals assume particular roles which allow them to deny a threatening alternative. So, a mother needing to feel different from her own restricting mother will be positioned as the indulgent one, enabled by her partner playing an exaggerated disciplinarian role. When this structure falls down under the weight of its own artificiality and inflexibility, the repudiated scene returns with a vengeance, mother faced with comparisons with her own mother, father falling like a plaster saint from his pedestal (Byng-Hall, 1981).

Case example: Don't mention it!

Amit (15) was a very high achiever academically, expected to sail through his GCSEs with high grades and to progress through to university and a successful career. However, he was referred in a depressed and agitated state, no longer attending school after having failed to complete his year-end exams, finding himself unable to draw his gaze away from random bits of paper on the floor, or other objects in his immediate environment. He had suffered this secret torture in other forms for a considerable time.

Amit was the only child of his widowed mother, a small, dignified, reserved woman, originally from Sri Lanka, a Jain by faith, and with a tendency to adopt philosophical postures about life and its problems. Her husband had died of kidney failure when Amit was 10. She did not at first report her husband's drinking problems which contributed to his death, nor the severe family conflict of which the drinking was a part and to which it contributed. Eventually, she spoke of her anger and disappointment in choosing a partner who would not act as a father should towards his son, and who lost his family the respect and support of their entire extended family.

She and her son now lived in a small but well-ordered world. Her attempts to make up for her late husband's deficiencies and to deal with her own loneliness drew her ever closer to her son, and yet she knew she must somehow make him able to cope independently. Her cautious supervision of his life plus her reserve and strong desire for his independence, based on her self-sacrifice, generated a binding paradox (stay close; move away; don't notice the difference). Amit's academic success would have made it likely he would soon move away; this and the whole process of his maturing threatened the family stability. His symptoms served to draw the outside world into the unchallenged world of their isolated and pained pseudo-intimacy.

Amit progressed significantly in therapy, having revealed a number of his own 'secrets', notably his homosexual identity. In a joint review meeting, Amit then 'accidentally' revealed his mother's secret, of bulimia, extending back several years. He had helped to hide his mother's shame for years, and described how mortified both of them had been when one day he had let the insurance man in while his mother was vomiting in the kitchen sink. In terms of life-stage possibilities, there was a stark contrast between a 'choice' based on ascetic, isolated, self-sacrifice, and another, moving beyond the rigid parameters regulated by symptoms, which allowed movement, creativity, and growth. The possibilities, comforts, and dilemmas inherent in these differing positions were then the stuff of therapy.

Families preoccupied by a child's physical symptoms

Families operating in denial of processes of emotional and relationship distress, and expending much energy, time and money in consultations to discover the physical root of the problem, are notoriously difficult to shift. Of course, proper diagnostic procedures to exclude the possibility of physical process difficulties should be pursued, but even where a distinct illness process is present, its significance for the family's functioning and general 'state' needs to be understood. Towns (1994), for example, emphasises the need for asthmatic children and their parents to find a voice in managing the illness: if they become 'docile bodies' in the hands of professionals who know best, the patient's very survival may be at risk. Even where no distinct illness or physical abnormality is present, a sense of personal control can be encouraged by, for example, personifying aspects of the problem and enabling the child to begin to enjoy bossing them about, instead of *being* bossed about (Wood, 1988).

It is important to take psyche, and soma, and system seriously, although once trust has been established the playfulness of creativity can challenge and disrupt the morbid intensity of symptom-focused families. Behind the presentation of the uniquely suffering child with phobic or psychosomatic problems, there will typically be a picture of phobic, obsessional or depressive difficulties in other family members. Such psychosomatic conditions may be seen as representing a 'constriction of emotional functioning' (Onnis et al., 1994, p.343), an attribute of a family system which 'has lost its evolutionary potential' (p.341), rather than a deficit of the individual. The family's 'choice' of a safe and familiar path, mythically conflict-free, has often been informed by past trauma and loss, making stability and mutual monitoring, organised on an involuntary basis around the trading of symptoms, an apparent condition for survival.

Such situations, where powerful demands are made at a non-verbal level, which are disowned at a verbal level, tend to generate paradox. Meanings of 'strong' and 'weak' become interchangeable as the person who cannot help making tyrannical demands depends on a vulnerable person who must pretend to be supercompetent.

To Prata and Raffin (1993) phobic patients are caught up in such paradoxical control games and, being 'unable to allow anyone else [including therapists] to declare themselves "one up" in their relations with them' (p.323), readily frustrate and defeat a succession of helpers: 'winning' and 'losing' (the opportunity for change) equally become interchangeable concepts. Stepping outside of the constraints of rigidified language, Prata and Raffin emphasise the need for the symptoms, based on family history, but maintained by powerful feelings to do with the offering and receiving of care in the present, suggesting that abandoning such a long-standing arrangement might be unwise. Onnis et al. (1994) offer an approach utilising family sculpting, 'a non-verbal method similar to the language of the symptom', in a way that reintroduces ideas about development over time, and which links bodily symptoms to the pains and constrictions of 'the entire family body'.

Griffith et al. (1989) propose six categories of mind–body interactions in order to systematically investigate physical or behavioural complaints, and thus to intervene in ways congruent with the data (and with family beliefs). Briefly, the patterns identified were:

1 *Neuro-behavioural patterns* – where the behaviour corresponded to an identifiable physical process; for example, in one case, 'bizarre sexual behaviour' proved to be related to a dementing process together with hypoglycaemia resulting from unstable diabetes.
2 *Psychophysiological patterns* – where the symptoms, for example of an irritable bowel, were affected by unresolved psychological distress.
3 *Autonomous patterns* – where the patients' response to the meaning and impact of the illness or disease (for their own and their family's future functioning) explained unstable moods, rather than this signifying further disease process.
4 *Captured symptom patterns* – where an illness such as anorexia is 'held on to' for its value in relieving antagonisms and holding on to the 'old order'.
5 *Detouring patterns* – where reports of the patient's deterioration signify an escalation of stresses in the family.
6 *Mimicry patterns* – where symptoms with no current physiological basis are employed to bring in help which cannot be asked for and which would otherwise not be offered: such symptoms may be copied from another person or from an earlier illness episode, and permit the 'sufferer' to collapse temporarily.

Patterns may exist at a number of levels, with attention needed for the 'real' depression, as well as help to address the context – for example, facing inevitable developmental changes, including the prospect of retirement and slowing down.

The symptoms of 'school phobics' might be seen to have been 'captured' by family interaction, often with powerful, intermittent displays of concern about the child's physical pains and distress. The concept of 'triangulation' (Wetchler, 1986, referring to the work of Bowen and Haley) is often invoked to explain the mission of the distressed child: 'when two members of a relationship are stressed, a third member is brought in to mediate the disagreement or defocus the primary twosome from the stressful situation'. The emergence of physical symptoms appears to remove any suggestion of family conflict, with any disagreements and tensions which do surface appearing to result from the attempts to help the child, rather than being fundamental to its condition.

Similar tensions can be acted out by closely-involved teachers, mirroring the positions of helpless anxiety and protectiveness on the one hand, and equally, powerless hostility and distancing on the other (Taylor, 1986). Where such processes are active, and particularly where there is a good deal of 'shopping around' (for example, to try to find a dietary or dyslexia explanation), it is crucial to clear the field if therapy is to have any authority and, thereby, effectiveness.

Case example: The girl can't help it

Wendy (12) was only too eager to tell me all about her pains and bodily functions (her bowels, etc.) within minutes of our first meeting at the tuition unit where I am a consultant. She had suffered from phobic school avoidance since she was about 9, and changes of school had not helped. She was now quite comfortable in the unit, and confident that she could never cope with an ordinary school again. I had been called in partly because she was so comfortable. Neither she nor her parents seemed to have taken in the message that this placement was a short-term measure designed to help her get back into mainstream education. Secondly, Wendy had been 'playing up' in the unit, complaining of headaches, stomach-aches, generally feeling ill, and demanding that her mother be phoned immediately to collect her. She had brought along various packets of tablets, but some staff thought she should have them whilst others did not. When I had met the staff group, I found them split down the middle in their attitudes towards Wendy, with one caucus viewing her sympathetically as a sick and upset child, the other seeing her as a manipulative 'little madam'.

It emerged that this split resembled the one present (but obscured) in the family and, indeed, in Wendy as an individual (her ideal coping self often despised the withdrawn and wimpish character she observed).

Wendy was a late child, and the only one from her mother's second marriage to a rather younger man, a hard-working builder who had had a deprived childhood and a very incomplete education. Roles were rather rigidly split, with Mother as the expert on Wendy, and Father as the breadwinner, seen as likeable and at times entertaining in the family, but with a low profile in terms of 'executive function'. Now and again, he would voice an opinion on plans for Wendy but would 'go over the top' or not be able to express himself clearly. Wendy would be upset by disagreements, and her distress re-engaged her mother as comforter. Wendy's body produced pains which let everybody off the hook: although these pains might be exacerbated by tension and stress, these and not family problems explained her school refusal.

Her mother could tell when Wendy was upset and would sometimes suggest her sitting down or taking a tablet, even before Wendy knew that she had a pain. Mother habitually reported Wendy's thoughts and feelings, and described her actions as 'we did such and such': sometimes Wendy would interrupt with irritation in her voice, only to tantalise by fully supporting her mother's assessment.

It was suggested that this 'ventriloquism' might need to continue until two sets of natural changes emerged: firstly, that Wendy herself would feel old enough to make sense of her own thoughts and feelings, and to express them; and secondly, that her parents would support each other in beginning to mourn the passing of the child-rearing phase and think about what differences might follow. As they stepped back from being helpful in the usual ways, Wendy would be freed to challenge her own habits and fears in an age-appropriate way.

Within a different timescale, externally imposed on both therapist and family, was the legal requirement for Wendy to attend school, or make other suitable arrangements. Both parents were coached in giving clear and unambiguous messages to support this process, and successfully established their daughter at a new mainstream school. In parallel, sessions using desensitisation, relaxation, and cognitive techniques helped Wendy to cope with school, to more generally function in groups, and to rebuild appropriate activities and social contacts.

Children of depressed, mentally ill or unstable parents

Sensitivity to a child's needs, coupled with timely and appropriate responses, are crucial factors in the early development of a child's security of attachment and sense of self. Proper development is liable to be severely compromised where the main carer is severely or chronically depressed or mentally ill, and appropriate alternative arrangements have not been made (O'Hagan, 1993).

Children in such situations can have great difficulty in understanding the transformations in mood and behaviour they witness. Older children find themselves having to take on responsibilities as carers. The parents themselves are likely to have had a background of childhood deprivation, and possibly of frank abuse; tend to show chronic tension and anxiety; have a general inability to exhibit warmth, caring and humour, or to be receptive to the same; are involved in repetitive marital or relationship conflicts, and may also live in unremitting poverty. In addition to their mental distress, many feel they have been failed by treatment systems still based on a predominantly medical model, where patients often report a sense of 'being their illness' rather than being encountered as unique persons. A small but growing movement of 'survivors' looks at mental ill health in terms of a broad 'disability' concept, which includes the recognition that prejudice, fear and inadequate services disable people's capacities.

Case example: Ups and downs

Annette (14) had not been to school for several months. Few teachers could recall her, but from the records there had been nothing to suggest a problem when she had been in school. One day she walked out, and she never came back. After a while, a group of girlfriends called at her house, but she sent them away. She became more and more isolated, and as each day went by, her problems intensified. Attendance at a special tuition unit was arranged, but again she stopped turning up, and her mother failed to initiate contact to explain why.

When seen at our centre with her divorced mother, Annette sat hunched and shapeless, cautiously watching proceedings from under a veil of dark hair. When induced to speak for herself (Mother having taken this on as *her* task), Annette told me with assurance, and yet in a 'baby voice', that she could not go to school, and that there was no point in doing anything because she was ugly. This was clearly not a matter for debate or persuasion.

Her mother, nervous and thin and plainly under stress, was only too keen to take the blame herself for not providing Annette with a proper (and present) father, for overlooking her while her older brother was in constant trouble, for never sticking to what she said. She had tried insisting on school attendance but was now too afraid to, because she believed Annette would overdose or run away (and in time she did both: her 'running away' involved a semi-deliberate placing of herself at risk of sexual attack, walking late at night alone across a notorious wasteland). In this way, she appeared to test the idea of whether she was desirable or worthless in a dangerous and paradoxical manner: she could 'prove' that she was attractive and in charge and that she was an ugly object of abuse simultaneously. She could implicitly ask for protection – from her mother, or otherwise via official intervention – whilst demanding to be left alone.

Annette wanted what she didn't want: how could we help her discover what she might want that was safe and ultimately life-enhancing? To do this involved tuning in to the anger of emotional abandonment which lay beneath the negativity. In a particularly highly-charged session, 'states' (such as ugliness, depression and silence) were reconnected to their message-transmitting purpose. It was then possible to provoke and assist conversations which rediscovered and charted the past; which dealt with roles and rules in the present (this included the re-involvement of Annette's father in the picture, first by correspondence, and later by regular weekend contact), and which considered possible alternative futures, a vista as unimaginable, at first, as the past was painful and irrecoverable.

The picture clarified into one of a depressed 'odd couple', always comparing themselves with some unreachable ideal and finding themselves wanting. They seemed to take turns as harassed carer and provocative victim in their helplessness.

Children who have suffered sexual abuse

The most serious long-term effects of child sexual abuse appear to be associated with penetrative abuse; situations where the abuse was violent or forceful; where it persisted over many years, and where, by virtue of it being intra-familial, bonds of trust have been severely damaged (Young, 1992). A range of very serious problems, often involving the unconscious strategy of experiential splits, has been noted, involving disassociation, eating disorders, drug and alcohol abuse, borderline personality disorder, sexual dysfunction or disinterest, depression, anxiety, rage, poor self-esteem, guilt, social isolation and a vulnerability to re-victimisation.

Such a victim is in an existential nightmare, both in relation to self and others, 'living in double reality' (Jones, 1991), unable to separate the perpetrator's 'loving self' from his 'abusing self', and with a need to resolve the problem relationship with his or her own body by abandoning it, and placing its experience essentially outside of the self. For this reason, cutting and other forms of self-mutilation, so abhorrent to witnesses, appear, as it were, to be perpetrated upon someone else. There is a significantly raised attempted suicide rate, and an even higher number of victims (4 out of 10) have thought of physically hurting themselves: 'They seem to treat the body with the same calloused disregard and cruelty, the same indifference to the value and sanctity of the human body, as the aggressor' (Sedney and Brooks, 1984). Their 'internalising symptoms', such as fear, anxiety and depression, plus more overt symptoms involving hypersexuality towards both peers and adults, can additionally leave victims vulnerable to re-exploitation.

Alvarez (1989) counsels the need for a particular sensitivity in therapy for children whose early abusive experiences have penetrated and fragmented their minds. An accepting and unhurried context is required to build up 'the mental equipment with which to think about experience' because of the necessary forgetting of trauma. Rather than being organised by an anxiety to force such memories to the surface, the therapist provides the opportunity for the patient to be a child in the presence of a supportive and non-abusive adult, creating a second chance for the developmental and cognitive stage-work which was damaged, lost or frozen in the abusive experience and its total context of denial of the child's status as a valid, feeling, human being.

Case example: Not me

Sabrina, an intelligent but intense mixed-race 10-year-old, was one of seven children referred to us from three different sources in one week, when her family appeared to be breaking apart. The older boys were ruling the household, with increasing violence: they had been encouraged to take charge, but now their harassed single-parent mother, Maria, of mixed Italian-Iranian parentage, adopted as an infant by an Irish couple, could take no more. As an agency, we too were overwhelmed – by the number and variety of problems presented to us.

A significant feature of this very complex situation was a powerful agenda concerning sexual abuse while the children were in Africa, having been abducted by their father. Features which relate to this theme are summarised below.

Motive (perpetrator characteristics):

- Almost certainly, there were more than one, and up to four abusers in two different countries (the children had been detained abroad for three years).
- While abroad, the father was said to have frequently brought prostitutes home: sexual activity would take place, apparently indifferent to the children's presence, or alternatively, to desensitise them to subsequent approaches.

Prior history:

- The father had always been evasive about his previous marriage, but for some reason was denied contact with his son and daughter from that relationship.
- There appeared to be a pervasive view that females were commodities.

Opportunity:

- Supervision: the mother, frequently under strain, craved peace and quiet, and would often prefer the children to be out of her sight, leaving the older boys in charge. They had been physically brutalised, and it appeared one or more had also been sexually abused. The mother had also not been present during the three years the children were abroad. In addition, the father and brothers were allowed to bathe the girls. Boundaries were left very unclear regarding who was in whose bed at night.

Vulnerability (victim characteristics):

- Age and development: abuse appeared to have started when the victims were developmentally immature, suggestible, and had poorly-formed language skills.
- Belief: Sabrina was frequently portrayed – by her mother in particular – as a liar and fabricator, someone who enjoyed getting others into

trouble, and even as a seductress. Therefore, it was highly unlikely that she would be believed were she to protest. Other attempts to communicate – for example, sexually explicit drawings – were seen as the products of her 'dirty mind'.

- Self-esteem: although of mixed white/Eurasian parentage herself, the mother considered herself white, and had powerful negative views about her black ex-husband's character, family and race. This, added to unmet needs for affection and status, lowered Sabrina's evaluation of her worth, and was thereby a further factor in her vulnerability.

In this case, as in so many involving sexual abuse, the child's personal development was compromised in a pervasive manner. Her identity, race and language had been denied; her ability to voice what had happened to her had been overridden, both by abduction and, most probably, by sexual abuse; her experience of being a child had been undermined by the requirement to be the 'good little mother' in place of a mother who might otherwise reject her (but did anyway); she had suffered multiple losses, including of her siblings to foster-homes many miles apart – and just when she began to contemplate a new future, her mother suddenly took her back again, a mixture between rescue and repeated abduction, compounding her confusion, and adding the loss of a caring foster-family to her catalogue.

Seen individually while still in foster-care, Sabrina completed a 'prompt-sheet' as follows:

Sometimes I'm afraid to ... *say somethink* (sic).
I don't like it when ... *people don't listen.*
It's hard for me to ... *think sometimes.*
Sometimes I wonder ... *what's going to happen in life.*

On another sheet, Sabrina suggested that the person who 'would not let me down' was her foster-mother, who by this time had begun talking, quite inappropriately, about permanency; Sabrina paused and added 'and Mum'. Two sessions later, at a point when Mother had suddenly announced her intention to resume the care of Sabrina and two of her siblings, Sabrina got up in mid-conversation, found the last-mentioned sheet, crossed out the foster-parent's name, and 'accidentally' dropped it by her mother's feet.

This led to a turning point in our work. We were forced to re-examine our agenda and personal feelings. Fortunately, we had built in regular consultation meetings with all who were professionally involved in the case. This allowed us greater clarity about dynamic processes not only in the family, but also in the wider system. Some potentially damaging, or at least limiting, scripts were:

1   to search for damage, or significant harm, which would fit in with a desire on the part of other workers to secure the legal powers to make permanent alternative placements for both girls;

2   indecisiveness, characterised by what film-makers call 'hose-piping', where the camera zooms in and out of the action so alarmingly that the viewer is confused, unsure where to direct their attention. In our case, there was a tendency to be drawn into scripts about alleged events in the children's past, and then to be thrown into the often chaotic transaction of the present – but with little 'depth of field' to see both elements as part of the same picture.

The children helped us to recognise our own confusion and anxiety and to interpret theirs to their mother. It was difficult to know what to say, and one was afraid to say the wrong thing. No one could think about the future until things had been said which would help us know what ground we stood on. This provoked some anguished discussions (and we were now able to withstand diversions into blaming the past, or current officialdom) before Sabrina suddenly announced that the only thing that would stop her having nightmares (of being abducted in the night) would be 'if Mum signed a paper that she won't send us into care again'. Touched, and perhaps taken aback, Maria's response was positive and direct. Sabrina had found her voice, and it was a voice that claimed an identity, a 'me' worth caring for, instead of a 'not me' that things simply happened to.

Subsequent conversations have opened up the area of Maria's conflicting feelings about her own adoption, her confusion over the place of men in her personal and family life, and crucially, how such themes connect to form a whole in current family process.

Conclusion

The concept of stress offers the possibility of drawing on a range of perspectives from across the human sciences. In working towards increasingly integrated understanding, we are doing no more than acknowledging the connectedness of living systems, discarding the quest to locate human distress in one exclusive location or particular domain. Within this past generation, a great deal has been learned about such connections: between cognition, attitude and behaviour; between psychological factors, illness and even the immune system; between family process and individual functioning.

I have attempted to describe a therapeutic approach which accepts the multi-level nature of stress, which gives attention both to the specific complaint and to its metaphorical messages, and which recognises the humanity of the therapist and the particular stresses of the therapeutic encounter. Such an approach aims to provide symptom relief, together with an opening up of possibilities in the direction of more satisfying and meaningful states of being and relationships. Stress, rather than being a single-channel persistent condition of anger, or illness, or anxiety, can be restored to its necessary place in the human condition, as a response to shock and challenge, and as a trigger to action and growth.

References

Alvarez, A. (1989) 'Child Sexual Abuse: The Need to Remember and the Need to Forget', in *Consequences of Child Sexual Abuse*, Occasional Papers No. 3, London: Association for Child Psychology and Child Psychiatry.

Andersen, T. (1987) 'The Reflecting Team: Dialogue and Metadialogue in Clinical Work', *Family Process*, Vol. 26, No. 4.

Anderson, H. and Goolishian, H. (1988) 'Human Systems as Linguistic Systems: Preliminary and Evolving Ideas about the Implications for Clinical Theory', *Family Process*, Vol. 27, No. 4.

Anderson, S.A. and Bagarozzi, D.A. (1983) 'The Use of Family Myths as an Aid to Strategic Therapy', *Journal of Family Therapy*, Vol. 5, No. 2.

Andolfi, M., Angelo, C., Menghi, P. and Nicolo-Cogliano, A. (1983) *Behind the Family Mask*, New York: Brunner/Mazel.

Anthony, E.J. (1986a) 'Children's Reactions to Severe Stress', *Journal of the American Academy of Child Psychiatry*, Vol. 25, No. 3.

Anthony, E.J. (1986b) 'Terrorizing Attacks on Children by Psychotic Parents', *Journal of Child Psychiatry*, Vol. 25, No. 3.

Ausloos, G. (1986) 'The March of Time: Rigid or Chaotic Transactions, Two Different Ways of Living Time', *Family Process*, Vol. 25, No. 4.

Ayalon, O. and Flasher, A. (1993) *Chain Reaction: Children and Divorce*, London: Jessica Kingsley.

Barker, P. (1993) 'The Child from the Chaotic Family', in Varma, V. (ed.) *How and Why Children Fail*, London: Jessica Kingsley.

Bateson, G. (1972) *Steps to an Ecology of Mind*, New York: Ballantine Books.

Beattie, M. (1989) *Beyond Codependency*, San Francisco: Harper and Row.

Black, D. (1989) 'Life-Threatening Illness, Children and Family Therapy', *Journal of Family Therapy*, Vol. 11, Special Anniversary Issue, pp.81–101.

Black, D., Wolkind, S. and Hendriks, J. (1989) *Child Psychiatry and the Law*, London: Gaskell.

Bowlby-West, L. (1983) 'The Impact of Death on the Family System', *Journal of Family Therapy*, Vol. 5, No. 4.

Bretherton, I. and Waters, E. (eds) (1985) *Growing Points of Attachment Theory and Research*, Chicago: University of Chicago Press.

Butler-Sloss, L. (1988) *Report of the Inquiry into Child Abuse in Cleveland 1987*, London: HMSO.

Byng-Hall, J. (1981) 'Family Myths used as Defence in Conjoint Family Therapy', in Walrond-Skinner, S. (ed.) *Developments in Family Therapy*, London: Routledge and Kegan Paul.

Campbell, D. and Draper, R. (eds) (1985) 'Adolescence in Families', in *Applications of Systemic Family Therapy: The Milan Approach*, London: Grune and Stratton.

Cohen, L. (1966) 'Stories of the Street', from *Songs of Leonard Cohen*, Project Seven Music.

Cox, T. (1978) *Stress*, London: Macmillan.

Crafoord, C. (1980) 'Put the booze on the table', *Journal of Family Therapy*, Vol. 2, No. 1.

Dadds, M. (1987) 'Families and the Origins of Child Behaviour Problems', *Family Process*, Vol. 26, No. 3.

Dale, F. (1992) 'The Art of Communicating with Vulnerable Children', in Varma, V. (ed.) *The Secret Life of Vulnerable Children*, London: Routledge.

Dare, C. (1993) 'The Family Scapegoat: An Origin for Hating', in Varma, V. (ed.) *How and Why Children Hate*, London: Jessica Kingsley.

Dell, P. (1985) 'Understanding Bateson and Maturana: Toward a Biological Foundation for the Social Sciences', *Journal of Marital and Family Therapy*, Vol. 11, No. 1.

Dingwall, R. (1989) 'Labelling Children as Abused or Neglected', in Rogers, W., Hevey, D. and Ash, E. (eds) *Child Abuse and Neglect: Facing the Challenge*, London: Batsford.

DoH (Department of Health) (1991) *Working Together*, London: HMSO.

Edwards, J. (1988) 'The Determinants and Consequences of Coping with Stress', in Cooper, C. and Payne, R. (eds) *Stress at Work*, Chichester: John Wiley.

Fishman, R. (1988) *Alcohol and Alcoholism*, London: Burke Publishing.

Freud, S. (1936) *The Problem of Anxiety*, New York: W.W. Norton.

Goldner, V. (1988) 'Generation and Gender: Normative and Covert Hierarchies', *Family Process*, Vol. 27, No. 1.

Goldstein, S. and Goldstein, M. (1992) *Hyperactivity: Why Won't My Child Pay Attention?*, Chichester: John Wiley.

Griffith, J., Griffith, M. and Slovik, L. (1989) 'Mind–Body Patterns of Symptom Generation', *Family Process*, Vol. 28, No. 2.

Heavey, A. (1990) 'Intelligence, Achievement and Gender: The Ramifications of a Case Study', in Perelberg, R. and Miller, A. (1990) *Gender and Power in Families*, London: Routledge.

Heisenberg, W. (1971) *Werner Heisenberg* (edited by Anshen, R., translated by Pomerans, A.), London: Allen and Unwin.

Hendriks, J., Black, D. and Kaplan, T. (1993) *When Father Kills Mother: Guiding Children Through Trauma and Grief*, London: Routledge.

Herbert, M. (1993) *Working with Children and the Children Act*, Leicester: British Psychological Society.

Hoffman, L. (1981) *Foundations of Family Therapy: A Conceptual Framework for Systems Change*, New York: Basic Books.

Johnson, K. (1989) *Trauma in the Lives of Children*, London: Macmillan.

Jones, Edward E. (1990) *Interpersonal Perception*, New York: W.H. Freeman.

Jones, Elsa (1991) *Working with Adult Survivors of Child Sexual Abuse*, London: Karnac Books.

Jones, Elsa (1993) *Family Systems Therapy*, Chichester: John Wiley.

Klosinski, G. (1993) 'Psychological Maltreatment in the Context of Separation and Divorce', *International Journal of Child Abuse and Neglect*, Vol. 17, No. 4, pp.557–63.

Kopp, S. (1972) *If You Meet the Buddha On the Road Kill Him*, Palo Alto, California: Science and Behaviour Books.

Laing, R.D. (1960) *The Divided Self*, London: Tavistock.

Laing, R.D. and Esterson, A. (1964) *Sanity, Madness and the Family*, London: Tavistock.

Lewis, C. and O'Brien, M. (1987) *Re-assessing Fatherhood*, London: Sage Publications.

Liepman, M., White, W. and Nirenberg, T. (1986) 'Children of Alcoholic Families', in Lewis, D. and Williams, C. (eds) *Providing Care for Children of Alcoholics: Clinical and Research Perspectives*, Pompano Beach, Florida: Health Communications.

Markham, V. (1990) *Helping Children Cope with Stress*, London: Sheldon.

Moran, P. and Eckenrode, J. (1992) 'Protective Personality Characteristics Among Adolescent Victims of Maltreatment', *Journal of Child Abuse and Neglect*, Vol. 16, No. 5, pp.743–54.

O'Hagan, K. (1993) *Emotional and Psychological Abuse of Children*, Buckingham: Open University Press.

O'Hanlon, M. (1991) workshop communication.

Onnis, L. (1988) 'Alcohol Abuse: An Interactional Approach', *Journal of Family Therapy*, Vol. 10, No. 1.

Onnis, L., DiGennaro, A., Cespa, G., Agostini, B., Chouhy, A., Dentale, R. and Quinzi, P. (1994) 'Sculpting Present and Future: A Systemic Intervention Model Applied to Psychosomatic Families', *Family Process*, Vol. 33, No. 3.

Patterson, G. (1982) *Coercive Family Process*, Eugene, Oregon: Castalia.

Patterson, J. and Garwick, A. (1994) 'Levels of Meaning in Family Stress Theory', *Family Process*, Vol. 33, No. 3, pp.287–304.

Perelberg, R. and Miller, A. (1990) *Gender and Power in Families*, London: Routledge.

Prata, G. and Raffin, C. (1993) 'A Cure Through Anger', *Journal of Family Therapy*, Vol. 15, No. 3.

Reps, P. (1971) *Zen Flesh, Zen Bones*, Harmondsworth: Pelican.

Ricks, M. (1985) 'The Social Transmission of Parental Behaviour: Attachment across Generations', in Bretherton, I. and Waters, E. (eds) *Growing Points of Attachment Theory and Research*, Chicago: University of Chicago Press.

Roethke, T. (1968) 'Plaint', in *Words for the Wind*, Bloomington and London: Indiana University Press.

Rutter, M., Macdonald, H., Le Coureur, A., Harrington, R., Bolton, P. and Bailey, A. (1990) 'Genetic Factors in Child Psychiatric Disorders II – Empirical Findings', *Journal of Child Psychology and Psychiatry*, Vol. 31, No. 1.

Schmidt, G. and Trenkle, B. (1985) 'An Integration of Ericksonian Techniques with Concepts of Family Therapy', in Zeig, J.K. (ed.) *Ericksonian Psychotherapy*, New York: Brunner/Mazel.

Seaburn, D., Lorenz, A. and Kaplan, D. (1992) 'The Transgenerational Development of Chronic Illness Meanings', *Family Systems Medicine*, Vol. 10, No. 4.

Sedney, M. and Brooks, B. (1984) 'Factors Associated with a History of Childhood Sexual Experience in a Non-clinical Female Population', *Journal of the American Academy of Child Psychiatry*, No. 23, pp.215–18.

Selvini-Palazzoli, M., Boscolo, L., Cecchin, G. and Prata, G. (1978) *Paradox and Counterparadox: A New Model in the Therapy of the Family in Schizophrenic Transaction*, New York: Jason Aronson.

Selye, H. (1966) *The Stress of Life*, New York: McGraw-Hill.

Sluzki, C. (1981) 'Process of Symptom Production and Symptom Maintenance', *Journal of Marital and Family Therapy*, Vol. 7, No. 5.

Solomon, Z., Mikulincer, M., Freid, B. and Wosner, Y. (1987) 'Family characteristics and post-traumatic stress disorder', *Family Process*, Vol. 26, No. 3.

Stanton, M.D. and Todd, T.C. (eds) (1982) *The Family Therapy of Drug Abuse and Addiction*, New York: Guilford Press.

Taylor, D. (1986) 'The child as a go-between: Consulting with parents and teachers', *Journal of Family Therapy*, Vol. 8, No. 1.

Terr, L. (1990) *Too Scared to Cry: Psychic Trauma in Children*, New York: Harper and Row.

Tomm, K. (1988) 'Interventive interviewing: Part III – Intending to Ask Circular, Strategic or Reflexive Questions?', *Family Process*, Vol. 27, No. 1, pp.1–15.

Towns, A. (1994) 'Asthma, power and the therapeutic conversation', *Family Process*, Vol. 33, No. 2.

Van Trommel, M. (1984) 'A consultation method addressing the therapist–family system', *Family Process*, Vol. 23, No. 4, pp.469–80.

Wallbank, S. (1992) 'The Secret World of Bereaved Children', in Varma, V. (ed.) *The Secret Life of Vulnerable Children*, London: Routledge.

Walrond-Skinner, S. (ed.) (1981) *Developments in Family Therapy*, London: Routledge and Kegan Paul.

Wetchler, J. (1986) 'Family Therapy of School Focussed Problems: A Macrosystemic Perspective', *Contemporary Family Therapy*, Vol. 18, No. 3.

Wood, A. (1988) 'King Tiger and the Roaring Tummies: A Novel Way of Helping Young Children and their Families Change', *Journal of Family Therapy*, Vol. 10, No. 1.

Young, L. (1992) 'Sexual Abuse and the Problem of Embodiment', *International Journal of Child Abuse and Neglect*, Vol. 16, No. 1.

Further reading

Behr, H. (1988) 'A Group Analytic Contribution to Family Therapy', *Journal of Family Therapy*, Vol. 10, No. 3.

Cooper, C. and Payne, R. (eds) (1988) *Stress at Work*, Chichester: John Wiley.

De Shazer, S. (1994) *Words Were Originally Magic*, New York: W.W. Norton.

Kermani, K. (1990) *Autogenic Training: The Effective Holistic Way To Better Health*, London: Souvenir Press.

Kolko, D., Moser, J. and Weldy, S. (1988) 'Behavioural/Emotional Indicators of Sexual Abuse in Child Psychiatric Inpatients', *International Journal of Child Abuse and Neglect*, Vol. 12, No. 4.

Liepman, M., Nirenberg, T., Doolittle, R., Begin, A., Broffman, T. and Babich, M. (1989) 'Family Functioning of Male Alcoholics and their Female Partners during Periods of Drinking and Abstinence', *Family Process*, Vol. 28, No. 2.

Muir, E. (1991) 'Integrating Individual and Family Therapy', in Szur, R. and Miller, S. (eds) *Extending Horizons*, London: Karnac Books.

Stratton, P. (1988) 'Spirals and Circles: Potential Contributions of Developmental Psychology to Family Therapy', *Journal of Family Therapy*, Vol. 10, No. 3.

Tomm, K. (1987) 'Interventive Interviewing: Part III – Reflexive Questioning as a Means to Enable Self-healing', *Family Process*, Vol. 26, No. 2.

Varma, V. (ed.) (1992) *The Secret Life of Vulnerable Children*, London: Routledge.

Varma, V. (ed.) (1993) *How and Why Children Hate*, London: Jessica Kingsley.

Watzlawick, P., Beavin Bavelas, J. and Jackson, D. (1967) *Pragmatics of Human Communication*, New York: W.W. Norton.

Worthington, E. (1987) 'Treatment of Families During Life Transitions: Matching Treatment to Family Response', *Family Process*, Vol. 26, No. 2.

8 Overview

Maurice Chazan

Introduction

This book has dealt with stress in various groups of children and adolescents: those with sensory impairments, physical disabilities, learning problems, emotional and behaviour difficulties, exceptional abilities, and those from ethnic minorities. Further, a chapter was devoted to stress arising from problems within the family, which may occur in any of these groups. Had space permitted, chapters could have been added on stress experienced, for example, by children who are victims of bullying (Tattum, 1993; Lawson, 1994); those who suffer the loss of a member of the family very close to them (Black, 1992), or children who have been involved in major environmental disasters (Dyregrov, 1991). These sources of stress have been referred to by contributors to this book in sufficient detail to highlight the main issues relating to coping with stress in childhood and adolescence.

The authors of the preceding chapters have had a difficult task in dealing with the topics assigned to them, for three main reasons. First, there is a very wide range of individuals, as well as a great variety of problems, subsumed in each of the groups specified. Second, the concept of 'stress' is not a well-defined one. As Rutter (1981) and Goodyer (1990a) point out, 'stress' lacks any agreed definition, and may refer to:

- a form of stimulus or stressor;
- an inferred inner state;
- an observable response or reaction.

Third, stress may occur at different intensities, and there are marked individual differences in vulnerability to adverse events, so that it is not easy to disentangle the relationship between cause and effect in any one case. In

general, the contributors have recognised these difficulties and have acknowledged the complexity between exposure to stress and a range of childhood
variables (Masten *et al.*, 1988; Cohen and Bromet, 1992). They have focused on
those experiences which are highly likely to cause distress and problem
behaviour in children.

This overview does not attempt a comprehensive summary of the seven
chapters, but will focus on five aspects of coping with stress in children:

1 causes of stress;
2 effects of stress;
3 preventing or minimising stress;
4 coping strategies;
5 future research.

Causes of stress

A wide variety of situations and conditions may generate stress in children.
As Rutter (1981) states, stress has come to include a very heterogenous range
of events, which may well have different psychopathological consequences.
Rutter also points to the difficulty of ascertaining, for example, whether
stressful events cause psychiatric disorder, or whether the presence of
disorder increases the likelihood of a child having stressful experiences.

In Chapter 5, Freeman emphasises that stress is unlikely to be due to a
single adverse event, but rather to an accumulation of stressful experiences.
This is so, but life-events may not have a simple, mechanically additive
causative effect: psychological distress (for example, in parents) may increase
the likelihood of a child experiencing stress (McFarlane, 1988). Many
researchers, too, have underlined the fact that the interaction between life-
events and emotional development is a complex one, and that many children
do not show evidence of emotional disturbance even when exposed to
chronic or acute adversity (Rutter, 1985; Berden *et al.*, 1990). Nevertheless,
Goodyer (1990a) points out that life-events need not be bizarre or cata-
strophic to cause psychological upset.

The causes of stress will be considered here under two main headings:
general causes of stress, which may affect any child; and causes of stress in
specific groups.

General causes of stress

The general causes of stress may be thought of in terms of (a) those life-
events which are likely to be experienced by most, if not all, children, and
(b) events which are less common, but which could happen to anyone.

Into the first category fall potentially stressful events which are likely to happen in the lives of most children – for example, bereavement in the family, temporary separations from a parent or from both parents, the birth of a sibling and a change of residence or school. Tensions occur from time to time in most families, which nowadays are increasingly likely to be affected by redundancy and unemployment, with consequent financial difficulties and emotional upset. Parental divorce has also become more frequent (see Chapter 7). The vulnerability of a child to stress may be heightened by fatigue, perhaps the result of staying up late to watch television. Going to school is an enjoyable experience for most children, but Moore (1966) and Yamamoto *et al.* (1987) have drawn attention to the stressful situations that many ordinary children face in adjusting to school. Such situations include inappropriate attitudes in teachers, over-pressure on children, a curriculum not suited to individual pupils, and being exposed to bullying (see Chapter 1). Entry to school may also be a stressful situation for the child and family (Elizur, 1986).

Into the second category come life-events and situations which are not so common as those listed above, but which are not confined to specific groups. These include a number of 'abnormal psychosocial situations' listed by Van Goor-Lambo *et al.* (1990). This list refers to abnormal intra-familial relation-ships, familial mental disorder or physical disability, faulty parental child-rearing practices and attitudes (for example, overprotection, over-pressure, inconsistency and rejection), the loss of a close love relationship, and sexual abuse (see Chapter 7). Not all single-parent families impose stress on the children in such families, but Fontana (1981) points to the strains experienced when a single parent must cope with a multiplicity of stresses – financial, occupational and emotional – and cannot avoid communicating his or her feelings to the child.

The contributions to this book have focused mainly on stress caused by factors within the home and school, but, as mentioned previously, some chil-dren have the misfortune to experience stress as a result of involvement in major disasters (McFarlane, 1988; Yule *et al.*, 1990) or in conflicts between or within nations (Fraser, 1974; Publishing Committee for Children of Hiroshima, 1980; Rosenblatt, 1983). Most children experience a change of residence or school, with or without consequent stress; but children from canal boat or Gypsy families are particularly likely to suffer stress and severe deprivation arising from their unsettled way of life and lack of continuity in their schooling, as the Plowden Report (DES, 1967) pointed out (see also Reiss, 1975). Serious difficulties in relationships with other children may also be a source of stress for any child: Goodyer *et al.* (1989) reported that friend-ship difficulties in the 12 months prior to the onset of emotional disorder were significantly more common in a sample of children referred for help on account of anxiety and depression than in a control sample drawn from the community (see also Coie *et al.*, 1990; Dunn and McGuire, 1992).

Causes of stress in specific groups

The causes of stress in specific groups have been discussed in detail in the preceding chapters of this book, and it will suffice here to make selected comments, drawing predominantly from the points made by the contributors, to highlight the main causes relevant to each of the groups considered. All the authors emphasise the difficulties in generalising about the causes of stress, even when discussing a particular group of children. As Steel (Chapter 4) states, the degree to which a child might suffer from stress is not intrinsically linked to any particular disability, nor is it necessarily associated with any specific combination of circumstances. Godfrey and Schreiber-Kounine (Chapter 3) also point out that the severity of an impairment does not correlate with the severity of stress created for the family involved.

Children with sensory impairment or physical disabilities Stone (Chapter 2), Godfrey and Schreiber-Kounine (Chapter 3) and Steel (Chapter 4) all show how stress manifests itself as a reaction to the restrictions and constraints which a sensory impairment or physical disability may impose on a child. Severe frustration is inevitable if a child has problems relating to mobility, co-ordination, communication or learning, or if he or she has to be highly dependent on others even to perform routine, every-day tasks. Some children, particularly those with partial sight, may be uncertain about the world to which they should belong. As the child grows older and enters into adolescence, the awareness of being different from others and possibly a sense of being less attractive and acceptable to peers tend to grow. The danger of a physically disabled child or adolescent, or one with a sensory impairment, feeling unworthy and rejected is considerable.

The tensions which occur in most families are likely to be exaggerated when they have to cope with a disabled child. The parents may have long-standing feelings of guilt or inadequacy, or they may harbour grievances against hospitals, doctors or local authorities; they may not be able to assess or meet the real needs of their child. The necessity for hospital treatment may mean frequent separations for the child, with consequent disruptions of the parent–child relationship. Siblings may not be able to adjust satisfactorily to the presence of a disabled child in the family. The stress generated by such family tensions is likely to be communicated to the child.

In school, too, the child's needs may not be adequately met, in terms of material resources, sensitivity of handling or access to an appropriate curriculum. The parents may be unhappy about the school placement, and may find it difficult to obtain the kind of education which they consider to be suitable for the child. In the mainstream school, the disabled child may have problems in adjustment to the peer-group; if placed in a special school, social contact may be restricted, with only limited opportunities for integration with children in mainstream schools.

There has been a growing understanding, in all sections of society, of disability in its many forms, mainly as a result of publicity given by the mass media, especially television. However, ignorance and prejudice have not entirely disappeared.

Learning difficulties Much that has been said above about children with physical disabilities or sensory impairments applies to those with learning difficulties, particularly if these are severe. Tilstone and Visser (Chapter 1) emphasise that experiencing learning difficulties makes children more vulnerable to the stresses and strains of every-day life. Failure is one of the main causes of stress, and constant failure is likely to lead to low self-esteem. Children with severe learning difficulties often have additional sensory, physical or motor disabilities, as well as retarded language development.

Within the family, a child with severe learning difficulties may present practical as well as emotional problems, with the need for special resources adding to the cost of living. Inordinate demands may be made on the time and energy of the parents. Schooling for children with learning difficulties may become a major source of stress if pressures are too great or if the child is a victim of bullying. In society, severe learning difficulties are still often seen as a stigma and a cause of embarrassment.

Children with emotional and behavioural difficulties The factors associated with stress manifesting itself as emotional and behavioural difficulties in childhood and adolescence have been well researched (Wolff, 1973; Rutter, 1975; Chazan *et al.*, 1994). Causes of emotional and behavioural difficulties may be related to temperament, medical/physical factors, home background, the school environment, the community and the peer-group. For a long time the child and the family themselves were thought to be the main sources of emotional disturbance. More recently, the school and community have received more attention as possible causes of emotional and behavioural difficulties.

Family factors include an unsatisfactory material and emotional environment, poor child-rearing practices, family dysfunction and rejection of the child. Stressful situations at home have been listed above and are discussed by Manning in Chapter 7.

School factors relating to emotional and behavioural difficulties include defective school policies and practices, teachers' unsatisfactory attitudes, faulty classroom management, learning difficulties and school absenteeism (Galloway and Goodwin, 1987). In recent years, teachers have come under increasingly heavy pressure as a result of a series of changes in the education system, mainly brought about by the Education Reform Act 1988. Their own stress may well communicate itself to their pupils (Travers, 1992).

Living in a socially disadvantaged neighbourhood where there is low morale associated with material deprivation may contribute to the stress felt by children (Chazan et al., 1977). Further, as already mentioned, being rejected by peers is likely to lead to unhappiness and possibly behaviour disorder of a disruptive kind (Dunn and McGuire, 1992).

Gifted children   Freeman (Chapter 5) poses the key question of whether gifted children suffer more stress than others in their daily lives because of their underlying problem of being different. It would seem that there is no precise answer to this question. Giftedness has its advantages and disadvantages in relation to emotional development. On the positive side, a high level of intelligence and competence in problem-solving are likely to safeguard the individual in stressful situations. There is no evidence to suggest that exceptionally high ability is of itself associated with stress and resultant emotional problems. Rather, as Freeman suggests, it is likely that children with a wide variety of mental coping strategies are less vulnerable to stress than others. Further, success – for example, in school – breeds self-confidence and a sense of self-worth.

However, on the negative side, gifted children do have particular problems and vulnerabilities. If they live in a community where high academic achievement is not seen as valuable, they may feel pressures from peers, or even from other members of their family, to direct their attention away from scholastic concerns. They may be bored at school if they are not given an appropriate curriculum and teaching. Expectations of them on the part of parents and teachers may be unrealistically high, or their emotional needs may be ignored while academic success is being pursued. Gifted children may also be aware, at an early age, of subtle aspects of family conflict, and develop a self-destructive over-sensitivity.

Children from ethnic minorities   By no means all children from ethnic minorities are exposed to adverse experiences relating to their being different in some way from the majority. Many lead happy lives in a closely-knit family and community, and many achieve success in school. In recent decades, society has become increasingly multi-ethnic, and people generally have become less xenophobic and more familiar with cultures and religions other than their own. Nevertheless, as Dwivedi points out in Chapter 6, in the UK more coloured people than white suffer from social disadvantages such as poor housing, lower-paid jobs and unemployment. There is evidence to show that racial discrimination and prejudice against minority groups have not been altogether eradicated (DES, 1985).

Children from ethnic minorities may suffer from the stress felt by their parents in their efforts to establish themselves in the community. They are also at greater risk of experiencing name-calling and being bullied in other ways, both in school and outside it (Gillborn, 1993), as well as of being discriminated against when they leave education to seek work. Particularly in adolescence, they may experience internal conflict, and possibly also conflict with their families in trying to adapt to the demands of their parents' culture at the same time as responding to the pressures imposed by their peers who belong to the majority ethos (see Gillborn, 1990).

Effects of stress

As previously indicated, the contributors to this volume have been at pains to acknowledge that there is no simple or precise relationship between causative factors associated with stress and their effects on any individual. Many children show no long-term adverse reactions even to chronic or severe stress. Reactions to stressful events and situations can be moderated by such factors as age, gender, temperament and problem-solving ability, as well as the family and social support available to the child (Rossman and Rosenberg, 1992; see also 'Preventing or minimising stress', below).

However, research studies have established that both anti-social behaviour and anxiety/depression may be caused, at least in part, by unfortunate life-events, adverse family conditions, problems at school or other stressful situations (Goodyer, 1990b). Such emotional and behaviour disorders may be long-lasting (Rutter, 1989; Robins, 1991).

Reactions to stress may be physical or psychological. Graham (1985) states that stressful life-events may lead to, or at least maintain, 'psychosomatic' disorders such as peptic ulcer, colitis and asthma. Stevenson et al. (1988) found that, in children as young as 3 years, recurrent stomach-ache or abdominal pain was an indication of a vulnerable child's response to stress. Anxiety in the face of threatening situations may result in a lack of sleep and a consequent inability to concentrate in school.

Psychological reactions to stress highlighted by the contributors to this book include withdrawal from relationships and perhaps into fantasy; temper tantrums; over-dependence, and regression to immature behaviour. Children under stress may resort to clowning in class, and even gifted children may underachieve in school or become aggressive towards others (see Chapter 5). Over-pressure by parents or teachers may lead to stammering, and chronic stress may result in delinquent behaviour or recourse to substance abuse or alcoholism. The authors have frequently referred to low self-esteem and a sense of unworthiness in children and adolescents experiencing stress.

Preventing or minimising stress

Stress cannot be prevented completely. Every child faces pressures at home, at school and in the peer-group. Some experience stress as a result of natural life-events such as the birth of a sibling or bereavement in the family. As Moore (1966) put it, frustrations cannot be eradicated from life, nor can all difficulties be smoothed away. However, in some cases, parents, teachers and peers cause unnecessary stress, or fail to deal adequately with problems likely to cause a child to experience stress.

We do not know precisely what factors act as moderators protecting children from undue effects of stress. However, research to date suggests that a positive, supportive family and school environment, problem-solving and social skills, and children's own beliefs about their control over situations do act as such moderators (Berden *et al.*, 1990; Rossman and Rosenberg, 1992). Goodyer *et al.* (1990) point out that a confiding relationship with a parent significantly decreases the risk of conduct disorder, even in the presence of marital disharmony. They also assert that close, affectionate relations with parents and the ability to maintain friendships seem to be important factors in the development of self-worth and personal competence.

Our knowledge to date of child development suggests, therefore, that any measures designed to help the family to function successfully, as well as a school policy directed at supporting children at risk of emotional disturbance or behaviour difficulties, will contribute to the prevention of undue effects of stress, or at least mitigate these effects. Such measures might include various forms of education for parenthood (Pugh and De'Ath, 1984; Wolfendale, 1992) and making teachers and others working with children more sensitive to the emotional needs of children and adolescents, through initial and in-service training (Hanko, 1990). Both the Children Act 1989 and the Code of Practice relating to special educational needs which supplemented the Education Act 1993 (DFE/WO, 1994) emphasised the importance of listening to children and taking into account their own views on their needs.

Themes given emphasis in this book include the importance of preserving children's dignity and comfort, developing self-esteem and avoiding a sense of failure, viewing disability and other challenges in a positive light, providing parents with adequate information and support, and changing the attitudes of society.

In Chapter 1, Tilstone and Visser advocate an adequately-funded programme of health education to ensure that the effects of ignorance and fear are alleviated.

In Chapter 2, Stone suggests that self-esteem and confidence in children can be developed through overcoming challenges from the early years: if children gain experience in social and problem-solving skills such as self-presentation and communicating to others, as well as coping with negative attitudes, their feelings of self-worth will be enhanced.

In Chapter 3, Godfrey and Schreiber-Kounine underline the need for early diagnosis of sensory impairment, adequate information and advice being given to parents, and a thorough assessment of the needs of the child and family. Helping parents to perceive disability positively is a vital task for the supporting services.

The points made by Steel in Chapter 4 in relation to physical disabilities also apply more generally. Steel lists a number of practical strategies likely to be helpful in the avoidance of stress, such as identifying situations which create stress for particular children, being prepared to respond to a child's anxieties and avoiding off-loading personal tensions and frustrations on the child.

In Chapter 5, Freeman advocates specific counselling help for gifted children and measures to eradicate stereotyping.

In Chapter 6, Dwivedi encourages the promotion of a multi-cultural ethos in schools, and of greater awareness of all forms of diversity in culture and religion. In his view, stress in minority groups will be mitigated by giving these groups every opportunity to develop their own communities and offer support to their members.

In Chapter 7, Manning, who points out that stress is not necessarily a negative phenomenon, discusses how family therapy can help children under stress. Easy access to professional help at an early stage is likely to help to prevent the effects of stress from being exacerbated or prolonged (see 'Coping strategies', below).

Coping strategies

Children deal with stress in their own particular way, and it is difficult to generalise about effective ways of coping with adverse events and situations. Rossman (1992) suggests that children should be helped to develop their own strategies, which might include self-calming, ignoring some situations, showing anger in a controlled way and talking to friends, parents or teachers.

Adults can help children to cope with stress by adopting a calm and empathetic approach, by using humour to defuse anxiety-inducing situations, and by modifying tasks to suit the child, as Steel recommends in Chapter 4 (see also Markham, 1990; Alsop and McCaffrey, 1993). It is difficult, but worthwhile, for parents and teachers to avoid getting involved in what might be termed a 'vicious circle'. Adults under severe pressure may contribute to a child being stressed and behaving badly; the child's misbehaviour is likely to increase strain and irritation in the adults, who may well treat the child harshly and exacerbate the child's hostile and unrewarding actions (Patterson, 1982; Robins, 1991). It is admittedly not easy for adults to be calm and constructive in such a situation, but in most cases, a positive approach will help to reduce stress all round.

Much can be done in school to prepare children for meeting the challenges of life. Class activities at all ages can include training in social skills aimed at increasing competence in dealing with others, insight into one's own behaviour and considering constructive solutions to every-day problems as well as to such experiences as being bullied (Cross and Goddard, 1988; Frederickson and Simms, 1990). Group discussions encouraging the skills of questioning, listening and managing disputes are useful (Tann, 1981). Tilstone and Visser refer to the Circle Time approach (see pages 13–14) which establishes peer support-groups to help pupils gain more control over their behaviour, express their anxieties in a safe environment and seek relief from stress (see also Mosley, 1993).

Over recent years, an increasing range of support services has become available for those children and adults in need of help beyond that available from parents and teachers (Davies and Davies, 1989). The child guidance and child psychiatric network, the school psychological service, school counsellors, family therapy centres and social services departments, in addition to various voluntary organisations, all provide support for children and families in stress. These services are generally available, though different establishments may offer different kinds of help. Godfrey and Schreiber-Kounine (Chapter 3) have discussed behaviour modification based on learning theory; cognitive behaviour therapy, emphasising problem-solving and the individual's own interpretation of situations; family therapy (also discussed by Manning in Chapter 7), and counselling (see also Campion, 1991). Some children may benefit from play therapy or other forms of psychotherapy (Rutter, 1975; McMahon, 1992; Cattanach, 1994), whilst speech therapists and physiotherapists also have a valuable part to play in relieving pressures on children.

Future research

As stated previously, considerable attention has been devoted by researchers to children and adolescents presenting emotional and behavioural difficulties, but few studies have been carried out on the effects of recent life-events on development (Goodyer *et al.*, 1986; Goodyer, 1990a and 1990b). Rutter (1981) considers that we need to know more about the relationship between exposure to stress in children and later emotional disorders; why and how individual differences operate, and the way in which stressful events may influence both the developmental process and also later functioning generally.

Other writers see the need for more research into such topics as:

- the moderating factors that influence a child's response to stress (Masten et al., 1988; Berden et al., 1990), including age and gender effects (Goodyer, 1990a, 1990b and 1991);
- children's perceptions of their ability to control situations – for example, parental conflict (Rossman and Rosenberg, 1992);
- children's views on what constitutes a stressful experience, and the incidence of these experiences through the eyes of children themselves (Yamamoto et al., 1987);
- the short-term and long-term effects of involvement in major disasters (Dyregrov, 1991; Yule and Gold, 1992).

There is also a need to know more about stress in children who lack stability in their lives because of frequent moves, such as those who are members of canal boat or Gypsy families, as mentioned above.

All the contributors to this book would endorse the need for greater under-standing of all aspects of stress in childhood and adolescence that would result from further careful and well-focused research studies. Publication of more accounts of effective work undertaken by practitioners dealing with children suffering stress would also be of great value in promoting such understanding.

References

Alsop, P. and McCaffrey, T. (1993) *How to Cope with Childhood Stress: A practical guide for teachers*, London: Longman.

Berden, G.F.M.G., Althaus, M. and Verhulst, F.C. (1990) 'Major life events and changes in the behavioural functioning of children', *Journal of Child Psychology and Psychiatry*, Vol. 31, No. 6, pp.949–60.

Black, D. (1992) 'Working with Children of Dying Parents', in Kaplan, C. (ed.) *Bereaved Children*, London: Association for Child Psychology and Psychiatry.

Campion, J. (1991) *Counselling Children*, London: Whiting and Birch.

Cattanach, A. (1994) *Play Therapy: Where the sky meets the underworld*, London: Jessica Kingsley.

Chazan, M., Cox, T., Jackson, S. and Laing, A.F. (1977) *Studies of Infant School Children, Vol. 2: Deprivation and Development*, Oxford: Basil Blackwell/Schools Council.

Chazan, M., Laing, A.F. and Davies, D. (1994) *Emotional and Behavioural Difficulties in Middle Childhood: Identification, assessment and intervention in school*, London: Falmer Press.

Cohen, S. and Bromet, E. (1992) 'Maternal predictors of behavioural disturbance in preschool children: A research note', *Journal of Child Psychology and Psychiatry*, Vol. 33, No. 5, pp.941–6.

Coie, J.D., Dodge, K.A. and Kupersmidt, J.B. (1990) 'Peer Group Behaviour and Social Status', in Asher, S.R. and Coie, J.D. (eds) *Peer Rejection in Childhood*, Cambridge: Cambridge University Press.

Cross, J. and Goddard, S. (1988) 'Social skills training in the ordinary school setting', *Educational Psychology in Practice*, Vol. 4, No. 1, pp.24–8.

Davies, J.D. and Davies, P. (1989) *A Teacher's Guide to Support Services*, Windsor: Nfer-Nelson.

DES (Department of Education and Science) (1967) *Children and their Primary Schools*, Vol. 1, London: HMSO (The Plowden Report).

DES (Department of Education and Science) (1985) *Education for All*, London: HMSO (The Swann Report).

DFE/WO (Department for Education/Welsh Office) (1994) *Education Act 1993: Code of Practice on the Identification and Assessment of Special Educational Needs*, London: DFE/WO.

Dunn, J. and McGuire, S. (1992) 'Sibling and peer relationships in childhood', *Journal of Child Psychology and Psychiatry*, Vol. 33, No. 1, pp.67–105.

Dyregrov, A. (1991) *Children in Grief: A handbook for adults*, London: Jessica Kingsley.

Elizur, J. (1986) 'The stress of school entry: Parental coping behaviours and children's adjustment to school', *Journal of Child Psychology and Psychiatry*, Vol. 27, No. 5, pp.625–38.

Fontana, D. (1981) *Psychology for Teachers*, Leicester: British Psychological Society.

Fraser, M. (1974) *Children in Conflict*, Harmondsworth: Penguin.

Frederickson, N. and Simms, J. (1990) 'Teaching social skills to children: towards an integrated approach', *Educational and Child Psychology*, Vol. 7, No. 1, pp.5–17.

Galloway, D. and Goodwin, C. (1987) *The Education of Disturbing Children*, London: Longman.

Gillborn, D. (1990) *Race Ethnicity and Education: Teaching and learning in multi-ethnic schools*, London: Unwin Hyman/Routledge.

Gillborn, D. (1993) 'Racial Violence and Bullying', in Tattum, D. (ed.) *Understanding and Managing Bullying*, London: Heinemann.

Goodyer, I.M. (1990a) 'Family relationships, life events and childhood psychopathology', *Journal of Child Psychology and Psychiatry*, Vol. 31, No. 1, pp.161–92.

Goodyer, I.M. (1990b) 'Annotation: Recent life events and psychiatric disorder in school age children', *Journal of Child Psychology and Psychiatry*, Vol. 31, No. 6, pp.839–48.

Goodyer, I.M. (1991) *Life Experiences, Development and Childhood Psychopathology*, Chichester: John Wiley.

Goodyer, I.M., Kolvin, I. and Gatzanis, S. (1986) 'Do age and sex influence the association between recent life events and psychiatric disorders in children and adolescents? – A controlled enquiry', *Journal of Child Psychology and Psychiatry*, Vol. 27, No. 5, pp.681–7.

Goodyer, I.M., Wright, C. and Altham, P.M.E. (1989) 'Recent friendships in anxious and depressed school-age children', *Psychological Medicine*, No. 19, pp.165–74.

Goodyer, I.M., Wright, C. and Altham, P.M.E. (1990) 'Recent achievements and adversities in anxious and depressed school age children', *Journal of Child Psychology and Psychiatry*, Vol. 31, No. 7, pp.1,063–78.

Graham, P. (1985) 'Psychology and the health of children', *Journal of Child Psychology and Psychiatry*, Vol. 26, No. 3, pp.333–47.

Hanko, G. (1990) *Special Needs in Ordinary Classrooms: Supporting teachers*, Oxford: Basil Blackwell.

Lawson, S. (1994) *Helping Children Cope with Bullying*, London: Sheldon Press.

Markham, U. (1990) *Helping Children Cope with Stress*, London: Sheldon Press.

Masten, A.S., Garmezy, N., Tellegen, A., Pellegrini, D.S., Larkin, K. and Larsen, A. (1988) 'Competence and stress in school children: The moderating effects of individual and family qualities', *Journal of Child Psychology and Psychiatry*, Vol. 29, No. 6, pp.745–64.

McFarlane, A.C. (1988) 'Recent life events and psychiatric disorder in children: The interaction with preceding extreme adversity', *Journal of Child Psychology and Psychiatry*, Vol. 29, No. 5, pp.677–90.

McMahon, L. (1992) *The Handbook of Play Therapy*, London: Routledge.

Moore, T. (1966) 'Difficulties of the ordinary child in adjusting to primary school', *Journal of Child Psychology and Psychiatry*, Vol. 7, No. 1, pp.17–38.

Mosley, J. (1993) *Turn Your School Around*, Wisbech: Learning Development Aids.

Patterson, G.R. (1982) *A Social Learning Approach, Vol. 3: Coercive Family Process*, Eugene, Oregon: Castalia.

Publishing Committee for Children of Hiroshima (1980) *Children of Hiroshima*, London: Taylor and Francis.

Pugh, G. and De'Ath, E. (1984) *The Needs of Parents: Practice and policy in parent education*, Basingstoke: Macmillan.

Reiss, C. (1975) *Education of Travelling Children*, London: Macmillan.

Robins, L.M. (1991) 'Conduct disorder', *Journal of Child Psychology and Psychiatry*, Vol. 32, No. 1, pp.193–212.

Rosenblatt, R. (1983) *Children of War*, New York: Doubleday.

Rossman, B.B.R. (1992) 'School-age children's perceptions of coping with distress: Strategies for emotion regulation and the moderation of adjustment', *Journal of Child Psychology and Psychiatry*, Vol. 33, No. 8, pp.1,373–97.

Rossman, B.B.R. and Rosenberg, M.S. (1992) 'Family stress and functioning in children: The moderating effects of children's beliefs about their control over parental conflict', *Journal of Child Psychology and Psychiatry*, Vol. 33, No. 4, pp.699–716.

Rutter, M. (1975) *Helping Troubled Children*, Harmondsworth: Penguin.

Rutter, M. (1981) 'Stress, coping and development: Some issues and some questions', *Journal of Child Psychology and Psychiatry*, Vol. 22, No. 4, pp.323–56.

Rutter, M. (1985) 'Family and School Influences: Meanings, Mechanisms and Implications', in Nicol, A.R. (ed.) *Longitudinal Studies in Child Psychology and Psychiatry*, Chichester: John Wiley.

Rutter, M. (1989) 'Pathways from childhood to adult life', *Journal of Child Psychology and Psychiatry*, Vol. 30, No. 1, pp.23–51.

Stevenson, J., Simpson, J. and Bailey, V. (1988) 'Research note: Recurrent headaches and stomachaches in preschool children', *Journal of Child Psychology and Psychiatry*, Vol. 29, No. 6, pp.897–900.

Tann, S. (1981) 'Grouping and Groupwork', in Simon, B. and Willcocks, J. (eds) *Research and Practice in the Primary Classroom*, London: Routledge and Kegan Paul.

Tattum, D. (ed.) (1993) *Understanding and Managing Bullying*, London: Heinemann.

Travers, C. (1992) 'Teacher stress in the U.K. – A nationwide survey', *British Psychological Society Education Section Review*, Vol. 16, No. 2, pp.78–82.

Van Goor-Lambo, G., Orley, J., Poustka, F. and Rutter, M. (1990) 'Classification of abnormal psychosocial situations: Preliminary report of a revision of a WHO scheme', *Journal of Child Psychology and Psychiatry*, Vol. 31, No. 2, pp.229–41.

Wolfendale, S. (1992) *Empowering Parents and Teachers*, London: Cassell.

Wolff, S. (1973) *Children Under Stress* (2nd edn), Harmondsworth: Pelican.

Yamamoto, K., Soliman, A., Parsons, J. and Davis Jr, O.L. (1987) 'Voices in unison: Stressful events in the lives of children in six countries', *Journal of Child Psychology and Psychiatry*, Vol. 28, No. 6, pp.855–64.

Yule, W. and Gold, A. (1992) *Wise before the Event: Coping with crises in schools*, London: Calouste Gulbenkian Foundation.

Yule, W., Udwin, D. and Murdoch, K. (1990) 'The "Jupiter" sinking: Effects on children's fears, depression and anxiety', *Journal of Child Psychology and Psychiatry*, Vol. 11, No. 7, pp.1,051–62.

Index

family
    definition 107
    dynamics 92
    problems 101–40
    scapegoat 112–13, 117–18
    sculpting 127
    session summary 115
    stress and coping 36
    styles and their impact 109–10
    systems 107, 109
    tensions 6–7, 66–9, 77, 144
    therapy 52, 102, 107, 108, 121
feeling 'different' 82–3
formal psychometric assessment 48–51
framework
    for gathering information about
        presenting problem 46–7
    for taking a comprehensive personal
        history 45–6
Freeman research 80–3
Freud 102
friendship bonds 14
frontal-lobe epilepsy 3
future research 150–1

gender and giftedness 79
genetic factors and alcoholism 122
gifted children 73–87, 146
global information schemes 9
'glue-ear' 35

'handicap' 59
handling and physical
    management 60–2
hearing impairment 35–55, 144
Hiskey-Nebraska Test of Learning
    Aptitude 50
HIV/AIDS 4–5
homeostasis 74

integrated placement 29
intelligence 48, 49, 73
IT (information technology) 64

labels 111
language 26–7, 42, 43

learning difficulties 1–19, 40, 64, 145
'learning difficulty', definition 1
levels of meaning in the family 104
Lightwriter 63
listening skills 42
litigation 67–8
locating stress 105–6, 135
low-incidence conditions 5

MacDonald Inquiry 93
mainstream provision for visual
    impairment 29
Makaton 13, 63
'mannerisms' 27
massage 6
'memory boxes' 15
Mencap 5
Milan school 103, 106, 111
minimising stress 148–9
mother–baby bonding 24
mothers 104
mourning for lost/absent vision 31
Multi-Cultural Teaching 93
muscular dystrophy 60, 69
myths 125

National Association for Gifted
    Children 80
National Curriculum 29, 30, 65
Neale Analysis of Reading
    Ability 50–1
needs of children with HIV/AIDS 4
Newham Monitoring Project 93
non-verbal communication 63

Orac 63
overprotectiveness 38

pain 5–6
paramountcy principle 114
parenting failure 112–18
partial sight 21, 22, 144
peer groups 40
phobic children 127
photophobia 22
physical disabilities 57–72, 144–5
physiological symptoms of stress 3